D1414396

THE EXECUTION PIPELINE:

A STEP-BY-STEP GUIDE TO MOVING YOUR BUSINESS IDEA FROM DREAM TO REALITY

BY ANTHONY M. FLYNN

Finish Well!
Anthony M Flynn

The Execution Pipeline: A Step-by-Step Guide for Moving Your Business Idea from Dream to Reality

www.executionpipeline.com

Published in Partnership With: Bedrock Creek

Cover Design: KQ Communications

Printed in the United States of America

First Edition: Fall 2015

Dedication

This book is dedicated to my amazing wife and children: Nikita, Taji and Alaya. You are my pride and joy. I am so grateful to have each of you in my life. I cannot imagine life without either of you and I am humbled by the fact that God chose me to do life with each of you. I look forward to many great years ahead as we all continue to fulfill our calling on earth.

Additionally, I dedicate this book to Nick Vande Steeg. Thank you for inspiring me to move in this direction. I have spent years watching you as a businessman, leader, father, husband, mentor and friend. I am so grateful that God allowed our paths to cross and I can legitimately say I would definitely not be where I am today without your love and support. Thank you for being an amazing man!

David Bader and Brad Fieldhouse, thank you for believing in me enough to consider me a partner in business. I am eternally grateful to have two brothers that understand capitalism through the lens of leveraging it for the sake of purpose and not solely for the sake of profit. To each of you, let's continue to change the world together.... one human being at a time!

Dr. Patti Ray, thank you for believing in me. Angela Atkins and Marlene Williams, I have tried locating both of you to no avail. Wherever you are, know that educators do matter and that you touched my life in ways you could not possibly imagine. I am grateful for you. Thank you all for choosing to be educators!

Acknowledgments

Thank you to:

Will Moore, Kemmons Wilson III, Dr. Stacy Spencer, Belinda Hardy, Dr. Larry Acosta, Carl LaBarbera and Dennis Neal. Each of you, named in the order in which I had the privilege of meeting each of you, has been exceptionally instrumental in my life in terms of my path to leadership. The skills I have developed and the challenges I have overcome can be directly attributed to what I have learned as a result of my journey alongside each of you. Thank you for believing in me!

To every investor, funder and community partner of my work, I am so grateful for each of you and am also very clear that nothing I have done would ever have been possible without your contributions. Thank you for believing in me, but more importantly, the missions I have been a part of for years.

To our Board of Trustees, Atlanta Advisory Board, leadership teams and staff of The Gifted Education Foundation and Bedrock Creek, thank you for believing in our missions, both being bound to "fighting for the underdog." We have been called to take this journey in life together and I am grateful that each of you has played a part in making this manuscript a possibility.

To my father and mother, know that I acknowledge the challenges each of you faced growing up and as a result of birthing me as teenagers. I am a statistical anomaly and society's projections did not define the outcome of my life. Thank you for doing the best you could with the limited skills and resources you had. I love you both. To my stepfather, thank you for being a great provider! I love you and will see you again! To my siblings, I love you all and thank you for the role you each have played and continue to play in my life.

Contents

Start Here!
Why You Need an Execution Pipeline

I don't know your story, but mine took an unexpected turn when one of the most successful leaders and businessmen on the planet inspired me to write this book. His story is impressive. Although his dad strongly influenced him, he didn't really have anyone guiding him as he grew up. He took the road less traveled, a journey that was anything but easy.

Nick Vande Steeg grew up in Southern California as the eldest of six children – *five* younger sisters. Although his dad worked hard to provide for the family, his mother had to stretch their meager finances to make sure they had meals. He graduated high school and spent the majority of his time surfing the shores of the Pacific Coast. Finally, after his mother challenged him to "do something" with his life, he shifted from being a self-prescribed "beach bum" to being a paratrooper in the armed forces, to a dedicated college student, and finally to being the leader of a $100 million division of a large company before the age of thirty.

He shifted from being a man who allowed life to toss him around to one who refused to let circumstances and conditions define his life. He obtained an Executive MBA from a prestigious academic institution, worked his way through the ranks of corporate America, and eventually became the CEO of a company that moved onto the Fortune 200 list under his leadership. During his five-year reign as CEO, the company grew to more than 65,000 employees and increased shareholder value from $20+ to more than $100 a share.

As I write this manuscript today, he stands as the patriarch of his immediate and extended family. He lives out his faith as a fantastic husband, loving father, and genuine friend to many. He calls me "friend," but in many ways, he has been like a father to me. I love him dearly and am certain that my life would not be the same without his engagement and support.

During a conversation over lunch at his ranch a couple of years prior to the development of this manuscript, he and I were reflecting on a time when I was only thinking of forming the organization that is now known as The Gifted Education Foundation. (Visit www.IAmGifted.org for more about this organization. We produce marketplace leaders from low-income communities across America). As he helped me think through some strategies to scale and expand the reach of the organization, he told me something that would change my life forever:

Anthony, I have been around a lot of great leaders in my life, but you happen to be the most disciplined I have ever met with executing on your commitments.

I was blown away. *Wow! I thought to myself, did he just say what I think he said? Did the man I look up to as a legendary figure in life and a global leader in business actually tell me that I am the most disciplined person he has ever met?* I was speechless.

His comment confirmed what I had suspected to be true — my Creator wired me to provide value to others in a strategic way: helping people move their business idea from dream to reality.

My mentor had accomplished what few people ever do. Countless people dream of becoming the CEO of a Fortune 200 company, but the truth of the matter is that only 200 out of 7 billion in the world each year actually fulfill this dream. Clearly, he had to jump quite a few hurdles; experience a lot of wins and losses; and review balance sheets, income statements, and P&Ls. Restless nights, angry employees, crucial decisions, and weekend assignments — he had to navigate all of it. He hired, trained, and worked with some of the greatest minds our world has ever known, the top 1% of executives, consultants, attorneys, engineers, and other professionals in big business.

Rather than cause me to become proud, his words about my ability to get things done humbled me. I had spent my entire life fighting an uphill psychological and emotional battle. Perhaps like you, I've wrestled with deep insecurities. His words of affirmation were one of the best gifts he could have given me, for they gave me great clarity about my purpose.

I had spent over seven years of hard work and accumulated thousands of dollars in debt to earn both a bachelor's and master's degree, yet I walked away from both still unclear about my purpose. Paying a lot of money for degrees doesn't guarantee success. But now I suddenly had a clear vision for how I could enhance the efficiency, productivity, and overall well-being of thousands of people — and through them, millions more.

The truth is that many seemingly successful people never find the answer to that burning question: *What on earth am I here for?* But once I knew my goal, I didn't know how I was going to accomplish it. His words inspired me to create a tool to help those with a passion for business, innovation, leadership and entrepreneurship. That conversation gave me the courage to share with others who battle with issues of procrastination and defeat. That day I decided to share my gift of discipline and execution to get things done. That moment I got up from the table, and I began conceptualizing this book — *The Execution Pipeline: A Step-by-Step Guide to Moving Your Business Idea from Dream to Reality.*

The metaphor of a pipeline represents the infrastructure needed to transport an idea, product, or service from one point to another. You don't need to buy expensive planning software or pay some advanced MBA student tons of money to write a business plan. The plan doesn't make your venture a reality. **Ideas don't self-execute.** The steps to long-term success lie beyond a business plan. This is why I wouldn't change a thing about my personal journey. The pain of my past prepared me for the path I'm on now.

I was a kid born to a seventeen-year-old mother. I managed to escape the poverty-stricken, self-defeating cycles many of my family and friends adopted. Despite the absence of my biological father while growing up and the presence of gangs, drugs, racism among other issues, I managed to accomplish something more.

My transformation defied the statistical norm. When I was younger, feelings of rejection and inferiority overwhelmed me, but I always got up the next morning and pressed on. I had desire, mentors, and God's divine plan — but so do many people who are unsuccessful. I escaped because I also possessed something intangible: *gumption.* At a certain point I had to actually execute on my aspirations. From taking the steps to move from point A to point B — and the struggles in between — I discovered the process I share in this book, the pipeline that turned my own business dreams into reality.

The mental, psychological, and emotional skills I needed to get through life are the same skills an entrepreneur needs to create and sustain a successful venture. According to the United States Small Business Administration, more than 90% of small businesses fail within the first two years. As they were for me, the odds are against you. You have to embrace this reality. According to Dun and Bradstreet, small businesses often fail because of weak leadership. In other words, if your business fails, you have to accept the part you played in that failure. So get ready for an uphill battle.

My goal is to prepare you for the battle. I have designed this book as a guide to help you wiggle your way into the 10% of ventures that beat the two-year death cycle. Although I wrote this book as a guide for launching a new venture (a non-profit organization, business, product, or service), many of the principles will transfer to your everyday life.

And remember: the key to a successful venture and a more satisfying life is to take action. Countless people get up every day and have an idea for a new venture, yet they never advance to the action steps. Instead of moving forward, they continue life as usual and end up dreading the next day. In this guide, I lay out the action steps so that, like me, you can beat the odds and escape from the harmful cycle that entraps you.

In the end, great dreams, lofty ambitions, and decorated plans won't propel you. You'll need drive, discipline, and commitment. You'll have to put in optimal energy and make sacrifices. I'm ready to take you on this journey. The question is this: *are you ready to do what it takes to see this journey through?*

I've divided the pipeline stages into two primary domains: *Theory and Execution. The theoretical domain* details the components of the pipeline necessary for creating external credibility. If you want to attract customers, investors, great talent for hire, and loyalty to your brand, you have to establish these foundational components:

- **Step 1: Developing a Focused Concept**
- **Step 2: Measuring the Concept Value**
- **Step 3: Creating a Long-Term Vision**
- **Step 4: Shaping a Short-Term Mission**
- **Step 5: Crafting a Strategy**

- **Step 6: Penetrating the Market**

- **Step 7: Defining Your Success**

- **Step 8: Differentiating Your Brand**

- **Step 9: Developing Human Capital**

- **Step 10: Assessing Your Finances**

In the *execution domain,* I challenge you to move your dreams (theory) into reality with **Step 11: Constructing an Implementation Plan.** A lot of books stop at theory without ever getting into the execution phases. You might hear this message from me a lot because it is so important: *ideas do not self-execute.* I'll offer you advice and prepare you for the journey, but, at the end of the day, you have to take the action steps. You have to invest the sweat equity.

So let's get busy!

"ARE YOU

"Are **you** ready to
do what it
takes to see

this journey

through?

READY?"

Step One:
Developing a Focused Concept

Step One:
Developing a Focused Concept

James Penney was born in 1875 to poor farmers. His humble beginnings and appreciation for hard work empowered him to work his way through the ranks of the Golden Rule store chain. He eventually purchased the chain and renamed it J.C. Penney. During the Great Depression, James personally took on more than $7 million of debt when the company lost more than $40 million. To add insult to injury, he nearly died when he was suddenly struck with tuberculosis. But his passion gave him the tenacity he needed to rejuvenate both his health and his business. He took out a loan, rebuilt the business, and ended up living to the grand old age of ninety-five. James Penney had a vision, the discipline to execute his vision and the resilience to press on through setbacks. He refused to allow anyone or anything to impede his long-term dreams.

Unfortunately, many people don't even get past the concept phase. Think about the last good idea you had. Have you pursued it or is it still on the backburner as you find yourself waiting on *the right moment* to move forward? You're not alone in this waiting cycle. J.C. Penney said, "Some folks have a wishbone instead of a backbone." The goal of this first step is to help you move from *wishing to working*. It's time for you to shift from conceptualizing to implementing.

To begin implementing, you'll need focus. You have to commit your energy to a single, clear goal. James Penney chose to focus on building a department store brand. You might have a million ideas flowing through your head, but to implement any of them you'll have to hone in on a single idea. Otherwise, as best-selling author Seth Godin stated, "You will become a wandering generality as opposed to a meaningful specific!" Resist the human tendency to become a wandering generality. The next ten chapters will help you select which of your concepts you should execute.

1 | Establish your Concept

The first thing you need is a clear set of blueprints. A written plan clarifies your process for both you and the public.

Carve out a few hours in your schedule to outline your ideas. Don't think so much about endless details that you end up empty handed and frustrated after hours of unproductive energy. Just write.

Once you've gotten out all your initial thoughts, set them aside for a few days. Return eventually and narrow your ideas down to 50-75 words. Simplicity and focus will help you shape a clear description for your audience. Once you've created the basic framework, you should edit your blueprints several times to ensure you've examined all angles.

The key is finding a healthy balance between free writing and careful examination.

[What exactly is your concept?]

2 | Discover your Inspiration

The best ideas solve a specific problem. What problem(s) are you attempting to solve?

The problem might be tied to something personal, such as escaping an incompetent boss, or it might be a wider-reaching issue, like helping an under-served group in the community around you. Whatever the case, take time to determine what drives you.

Once again, the key is to write it out. If you don't get it on paper, it will lack clarity. If it's not clear, it will never become reality.

After you've clarified your plan, you'll need to remember your inspiration. When external factors challenge and overwhelm you, this inspiration will keep you going. Remind yourself that the pain of going backward outweighs the pain of pressing forward. Ultimately, pressing forward leads to a definitive solution.

[What inspired your concept in the first place?]

3 | Align the Concept with Your Core Values

Almost every successful leader I know spends his or her time investing in activities that align with specific core values. Clear core values will guide your major decisions and help you maintain your focus.

Take some time now to define four to six non-negotiable core values and commit to them.

As you define your values, you might make some difficult discoveries. You might find that you've wasted time, lived an undisciplined life or followed the advice of unqualified guides. Pay close attention to these issues because they will follow you if not addressed.

 When these issues threaten to hold you back on your journey, you'll need to hold on to your core values. Let your values guide and focus you while pursuing your dreams.

How does your concept align with your core values?

4 | Prepare to Sacrifice

You might have an excellent idea, but millions of other people in this world have great ideas, too. Of these millions of good ideas, only a few pass the implementation test, and even fewer last more than a few years.

Even successful businesses can lose traction over time. A large percentage of Fortune 500 companies die within a decade of having reached their pinnacle of success. To avoid failure, you'll need to make long-term sacrifices. Developing and sustaining a venture of any kind requires undivided attention, and you'll have to reorganize your life, perhaps even letting go of some figments of loyalty to other things.

Regardless of your previous experience, if you're a new entrepreneur you have never done anything like THIS before. Ask yourself now what price you're willing to pay for the success of your venture and compare this to your current priorities.

- Are you currently employed?
- Are you married?

- Do you have a family?
- Are you a single mother or father?
- Are you enrolled in school?
- Are you financially strapped?

You'll need to consider questions like these before you take the leap forward. Otherwise, you might discover too late that the sacrifices are too great.

What will you have to give up to proceed with this concept?

5 | Assess your Motives

Imagine a billionaire invested in your concept so that you never had to work another day in your life. Would you still get up every day with the same enthusiasm for your venture?

If the answer is a resounding *yes,* you are definitely moving in the right direction. If the answer is no, you might want to reflect on your inspiration for moving forward.

Although you won't always love everything about your work, you should evaluate your motives. Don't pursue a venture for money or special perks. Trail-blazing a new idea is not always glamorous and your passion will often be the only incentive you have.

What did Dr. Martin Luther King, Jr., Bill Gates, Oprah Winfrey, and Steve Jobs have in common? Passion. Don't underestimate the power of passion and its ability to keep the engine turning when times get hard.

Each of the aforementioned individuals had to struggle. Don't think for a moment that they achieved what they did without some significant challenges. Second, they had enough passion for their missions to push through those struggles.

Many of the greatest products, businesses and services began as someone's passion. In most cases, these entrepreneurs would pursue these passions even if they weren't compensated for them.

Do something you would do for free. Then figure out a way to get paid for it.

How hard would you work to implement this concept for free?

6 | Consider Your Qualifications

The "10,000-hour rule" says you have to spend eight to ten years (depending upon the number of hours you work each week) honing a skill. If you can bind your new venture to a skill you've practiced the last decade of your life, your odds of success increase. Success is still not guaranteed, but the odds of success in a venture are stronger when you've invested thousands of hours perfecting the skills needed to be considered an expert in a particular area of focus.

Young phenomenons like Mark Zuckerberg (Facebook founder) or Justin Bieber (musical artist) have made sudden success seem possible. Along with that, today's social media culture also gives these celebrities the appearance of overnight success. In reality, even they spent years perfecting their craft. Justin Bieber started playing drums when he was about 4 years old.

I argue that the typical "overnight success story" takes approximately ten years to build. So if you haven't already invested a significant amount of time becoming an expert in your area of interest, you can expect a lot of long hours, sleepless nights and mistakes along the way. It comes with the territory of success in this capacity.

Once you choose to develop a particular set of skills, you can use these to differentiate yourself from your competitors. The bottom line is you have to take time to think about what makes you an expert in the space where you're competing.

Why do you think YOU are the best person to implement this concept?

7 | Leverage Your Competitive Advantages

If you're anything like me, you're running too fast to stop and evaluate your accomplishments, but you should never rush past statistics that could influence your future success. Although your sights should focus on the future, you should keep the past somewhere in the periphery. As the saying goes, history can be indicative of future success. If you don't track your history, you have no benchmarks to measure your capacity for future success.

Don't become so obsessed with your accomplishments, however, that you fail to innovate, create and work harder than your competitors. If you ever forget these qualities, your venture will suffer. You know the devastating effects of self-satisfaction if you've ever sat with someone who spends all of his time talking about his success. People who've actually done what they talk about don't have to spend time convincing others of what they have accomplished. If you constantly fight to stay ahead of your competitors, your success will speak for itself.

Carve out some reflection time to list your personal offerings and assets. Do this at least every quarter, although monthly or weekly assessment might be necessary. You don't want to steal time away from high-level production just to build yourself up, but you need the time away from the hands-on work to ensure that you're documenting information that can contribute to your business.

In the non-profit world, for example, statistics are everything. If you're not capturing metrics, you're essentially non-existent. As evidence, entire teams, divisions and even companies exist for the sole purpose of capturing non-profit's success stories and metrics. Long-term sustainability depends on this type of documentation, as funders require evidence of progress.

When calculating your metrics and determining your greatest assets, start with your competitive advantages. Some possible advantages you might have include any successful projects or businesses you've started, initiatives you've piloted, education, work history, community service, or noteworthy connections. Assets can even include mistakes or challenges if you have empirical or anecdotal data to show how you overcame them.

Take some time to make a list of your greatest assets along with your competitive advantages. Then, when you're competing for a large contract, submitting an application for a large grant or aiming to lure a large customer away from a competitor, you'll know just what to emphasize.

What are the competitive advantages you can leverage?

8 Determine Your Goals

The Apostle Paul, in the Bible, wrote a farewell letter to a group of people in the city of Ephesus. He warned them how important it was for them to make a difference in the world. Paul's message explains why he chose the life of a missionary:

> You yourselves know that these hands ministered to my own needs and to the men who were with me. In everything I showed you that by working hard in this manner you must help the weak and remember the words of the Lord Jesus, that He Himself said, 'It is more blessed to give than to receive.' (Acts 20:34-35)

Paul wanted the people of Ephesus to understand the importance of hard work, but not simply for the sake of hard work or financial return. He wanted them to work hard so they could change lives. Like Paul, you too have the opportunity to make a pivotal change. You simply need the courage to begin the process.

My advice: don't wait another second to pursue something meaningful. You can find work that allows you to feed your family and still experience intrinsic fulfillment as you impact the world around you. One of the primary reasons people fail to make a career change is because their visions stop at simply earning enough to pay the bills. They get comfortable. Successful entrepreneurs see a problem they want to solve and take action to solve it. They seek more than status quo, a mediocre life or a job that simply pays the bills. They accept the challenge of entrepreneurship because something greater than profit drives them.

By no means should you quit your job tomorrow, but you can begin preparing mentally today. Start by creating a one, two or three-year transition plan that supports your goal for making a difference in the world around you. Identify what's driving you and chase it. You don't have to sprint, but begin stepping toward your dream.

Set a date, develop some metrics, create a plan of action and pursue that goal. (You'll get more guidance on this process as we journey together through this book.)

What impact do you want to make?

"Don't **wait** another **second** to pursue *something* *meaningful.*"

Step Two:
Measuring the Concept Value

Step Two:
Measuring the Concept Value

When starting a new venture, you'll need to create a value proposition. A value proposition is an easy-to-follow plan that convinces financers and customers that your concept is worthwhile.

To do this, you'll need to know your audience and what troubles them. Once you know the issues, you need to determine whether your concept resolves these issues. If you don't have the resources, infrastructure, or experience to address the problems, you shouldn't pursue that path. Entering an arena unprepared will increase the likelihood that your competitors will devour you.

When developing your value proposition, remember that your goal shouldn't be to provide the same value as your competitors. You should provide more value. Your value proposition is meant to persuade your audience to choose your concept over your competitors. With that goal in mind, keep your proposition clear and concise, and include quantifiable evidence that shows your superiority.

Don't underestimate the importance of this step. The ability to articulate your value proposition, or the lack thereof, can show you a lot about your chances of success.

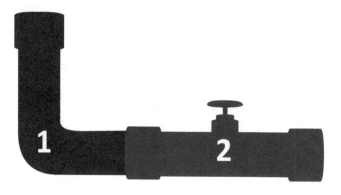

9 | Assess the Need

When determining your concept's value, you have to consider whether another product or service already solves the problems you're concentrating on. Consumers already have a million options to choose from when making a purchase. The last thing you want to do is confuse the market more by making it a million and one.

If similar concepts exist, your one chance to chip away at market share is to grow such an outstanding business that consumers default to your brand. However, in order for that to happen, you have to offer unquestionable value. For example, if you're developing a social media app, ask why a consumer would leave other popular apps to use yours. If you plan to monopolize the chocolate chip cookie market, what unique quality prevents a big-box producer from replicating your brand and smothering you? Consumers have to make a choice, and your goal is to make sure your product or service wins their dedication. If you simply replicate the work of your competitors, you'll fail. You'll lack legal and financial backing, proper branding, and—most importantly—customers.

You must have a differentiating value so obvious that your consumers can't help but convert to your product or service.

Is your problem already being solved by someone else?

10 | Position Yourself Strategically

Think about YOU. Consider how YOU and YOUR idea will offer a differentiating value to the market you aim to penetrate. Be painfully honest about whether you're the best person to bring this idea, product, or service to market. The most innovative thinkers are not always the best concept implementers and the best implementers are not always the best investment pitchers. You might have an awesome idea for saving whales, but with limited to no experience in marine life, you might not be the best person to execute that idea.

If you have the time and determination to become an expert in the field, go for it. If you plan to launch next year, however, you should reconsider.

Bob Shank, a mentor of mine and the founder of The Master's Program (www.mastersprogram.org), once told me that there are three types of people:

- **Originators** — They constantly have new ideas and thrive on the start up process.

- **Organizers** — They take the originators' ideas and give them the structure to stand long-term.

- **Operators** — They guide concepts once they're established and ready to be institutionalized.

Although a single individual might have the capacity to dabble in all three, they'll rarely be able to sustain all three long-term.

You'll need to be honest with yourself and find the category in which you fit best. You might want to ask some friends or mentors which category they see you in. You would rather be brutally honest now than to launch your idea and see it fall apart later. Determine if YOU are the best leader for the job.

Where should you strategically position yourself to best move your venture forward?

11 | Identify Your Concept's Benefits

Consider what you have to offer the market and why a consumer would continue to choose your product or service over another.

You will need a comprehensive understanding of your competitive advantage and your competition's disadvantage. Healthy competition will empower you to compare your strengths and weaknesses to others. However, it is important to keep in mind that you don't want to spread bad publicity about your competitor in order to capture a share of the market. If a company's leadership has ethical flaws, consumers might wonder if the product or service has quality flaws. On the other hand, if a product or service has high quality, the odds of generating customer loyalty from consumers strengthens. Ultimately, market share sales will offer all the evidence you need.

FedEx offers an example of healthy competition. They focus on the timeliness of their deliveries without disparaging their competitors. FedEx doesn't just ship goods; they sell convenience. They market this differentiating advantage with a formula that you can imitate: "They [your competitor] do X, but we [your brand] do X better," or "They do X, but we do Y."

Competing in the non-profit world is even more difficult, but it's still possible. If your concept serves a challenged demographic, such as low-income communities or victims of human trafficking, you don't want to put others out of business. You can, however, find a creative edge and strengthen the work already taking place.

You can set yourself apart from your competition and still maintain your integrity. Begin with the end in mind. Then think about how your idea offers a new and improved solution for the consumer's problems.

What benefit are you providing to the world around you?

12 | Provide a Unique Strategy

As you think about penetrating a market that already exists, you'll need to think of how you can set yourself apart and secure market share. Your approach to differentiation has to be clever, attractive, cost-effective, sustainable and delivered with excellence.

Almost anywhere you travel, you face thousands of lodging options, but none compare to the prestigious Ritz-Carlton hotels. This chain is the only company to win the Malcolm Baldridge National Quality Award twice, and Training Magazine voted it best in the nation for employee training. While the Ritz-Carlton competes in an industry full of alternatives, they've established a unique value proposition.

One way the Ritz sets itself apart is with its motto: "We are ladies and gentlemen, serving ladies and gentlemen." The company treats its employees like royalty, and they in turn treat their guests like royalty. The practice behind the motto elevates the experience guests have when interacting with staff at the Ritz. From the bellmen at the entrance to the floating staff members perusing the lobby for someone to assist, every staff member wears a smile.

The Ritz gained its prestige because it recognized the value market cause and effect: people pay for what they value, and they value whatever solves their problems best. The Ritz can charge their customers more because their customers see the value in the hotel's service. Whatever arena you hope to enter, create and highlight a unique delivery strategy. Great ideas will remain just that—great ideas—unless you have an execution plan. Be sure you match the inspiration of your ideas with an actual strategy for delivery.

Do your research. Study others who've successfully risen above the competition. Deliberate on trials and triumphs that made them successful. Then, take that information and create a plan.

How will you deliver a unique benefit to the world around you?

13 | Ensure Concept Propriety

A proprietary idea is one that is exclusively yours. A person can only use a proprietary product if they purchase or license it from the creator. The purchase can be as simple as buying a book, essentially purchasing the intellectual property of the author. Another form of licensing is proprietary property licensing. This process allows the original owner to benefit from the licensee's desire to utilize the intellectual property. School systems have been known to leverage proprietary property licensing in order to utilize curricular offerings in classrooms. Usually, those that are most successful are those that add substantial value to the academic curriculum already offered to students. Life skills, sex education, financial literacy and post-secondary career training are examples of curricular offerings that come in the form of proprietary property licensing.

As you think about bringing your concept to life, make sure the idea doesn't already have a copyright, trademark, or patent owned by someone else.

Not sure what they are? See my definitions of each below:

- **Copyright** – a legal concept that grants the originator exclusive usage to its rights and distribution.

- **Trademark** – a design or expression that identifies a product or service as distinct from a competitive product or service.

- **Patent** – an exclusive right(s) granted to an owner, inventor, or creator in exchange for detailed, public disclosure of an invention.

These simplified definitions don't cover everything, of course. I recommend you do extensive research on these three categories and consider contacting an attorney who specializes in at least one, if not all of these areas.

Do your research and be sure you're prepared to defend your own concept's propriety rights or your claim to a purchased or licensed idea.

Is your concept proprietary?

14 | Educate Your Audience

Before starting a new venture, you should research whether a market already exists for your product or service. If there is a market, consider how much energy, time, and capital you'll need to invest to penetrate that market.

Usually, the first company to successfully penetrate a market has the greatest leverage to capture sustaining market share in the long-term. If a monster business already exists in the market, they'll likely stifle your venture before you gain momentum. For example, you might have a great soft drink idea, but even if you can penetrate the market, Coke and Pepsi will forever dominate your product. Both companies see billions of dollars in revenues annually, giving your product little chance in the competition.

Count your costs and know exactly what you're getting into when you decide to compete with existing giants in a market. You might be the next Steve Jobs or Bill Gates, an inventor of an idea or service that revolutionizes the global economy, but those odds are about 1:7 billion.

To make your venture a success, you'll need to keep a realistic mindset, but you also need to believe in your idea. Expect the best, but plan for the worst.

If you do your research and discover the market you're attempting to penetrate doesn't exist, you have a huge opportunity to create a market. Prepare yourself.

Calculate how much time, money, human capital and hard work you think you'll need. Then double your expectations. Your expectations only account for what you plan, but start-ups experience many unexpected demands.

Whether you're attempting to penetrate an existing market or create a new market, get ready to take the road less traveled. Along the way you'll experience triumphs, but you'll also face trials. Crises will test your character and your dedication to your venture. You face a major undertaking when preparing to educate a new market. Don't be disheartened though. Many of the greatest risks in history have produced the greatest returns on investment.

How much will you have to educate your target audience?

APPROACH

"Your **approach** to differentiation **has** to be clever, *attractive*, *cost-effective*, **sustainable** & *delivered with* **excellence**.

EXCELLENCE

Step Three:
Shaping a Long-Term Vision

Step Three:
Shaping a Long-Term Vision

Throughout the journey, your venture will have two withstanding guides: a vision statement and a mission statement. Although the two sound similar, they have important distinctions. Your mission statement reflects your current state, while your vision captures your company's overarching focus for the future.

One way to think about this difference is to imagine the vision as the journey and the mission as the various paths you take to make the journey. Mission statements often have attainable goals and can change over time. Vision statements, on the other hand, will generally persist in the same form. The vision forms the core of your venture, a reminder of what your company or concept is about. Another way to think about it is that the vision statement represents your *being* while the mission statement represents your *doing*.

For a more concrete illustration of this difference, imagine a person arriving in New York City for the first time to explore the city in just three days. He lands at JFK and discovers he's forgotten to arrange for transportation. He knows his vision (to see as much of New York City as possible in three days). However, to achieve this he has to develop a plan, also known as a mission. A mission statement for this scenario might be to utilize three modes of transportation in order to experience various cultural elements of New York City. Once our imaginary tourist has established this general plan, he can begin filling in the details, choosing which modes of transportation to use, which cultural elements to see, etc. These details form the tourist's strategy, which we'll discuss more in later chapters.

As you can see, the parts are interconnected: the vision provides a framework for the mission, the mission provides a framework for the strategy, the strategy influences the implementation, implementation produces results, and results point you to your ROI as a business or impact as a non-profit organization.

Now that we can differentiate between mission statements and vision statements, let's look at how you can shape your own statements. In this section, we'll focus on creating an effective vision statement.

15 | Identify Your Long-Term Goals

Think about how you want the end of your venture to look and how you want people to remember it. If you had five minutes to tell the world what your business will accomplish long-term, what would you like to say?

Your concept will change during the journey, and your desired ending will probably change with it. Through it all, however, you should maintain a consistent, overarching vision. One of the greatest examples of a withstanding vision is the "I Have a Dream" speech Dr. Martin Luther King, Jr. delivered:

> And so even though we face the difficulties of today and tomorrow, I still have a dream. It is a dream deeply rooted in the American dream.
>
> I have a dream that one day this nation will rise up and live out the true meaning of its creed: "We hold these truths to be self-evident, that all men are created equal." ...
>
> And when this happens, and when we allow freedom to ring, when we let it ring from every village and every hamlet, from every state and every city, we will be able to speed up that day when all of God's children, black men and white men, Jews and Gentiles, Protestants

and Catholics, will be able to join hands and sing in the words of the old Negro spiritual:

Free at last! Free at last!

Thank God Almighty, we are free at last!

King's journey to fulfill his dream took many undesirable turns that forced him to change the plan's finer details. Yet, the dream became reality. Despite the detours, King remained loyal to his vision and obtained his desired end. Think about your dream(s) and the impact you want to make on the world long-term. Begin writing down your thoughts so you can use them when you finalize your vision statement.

What are you trying to accomplish long-term?

16 | Clarify the Core of Your Long-Term Vision

You need integrity when defining the core of your vision. In this case, integrity means full devotion to your implementation plan. If you proclaim a vision publicly and fail to follow through, you can create a whole slew of unnecessary troubles for yourself.

You want to have a clear vision before you go public. The last thing you want to do is proclaim one thing to the world, begin building your framework off that proc-lamation, and then realize you intended something else. While you can and will likely have to make adjustments along the way, keep within the guardrails you set with your vision statement. Many of the greatest concepts never come to fruition because the implementers lose sight of the venture's core, and the project loses structure as a result.

To avoid derailing, you'll need to determine your end desire. This clarity becomes your guide through every decision, from employment decisions to growth strategy. Here's the good news: once you have a clear core vision, you and your team can get as creative as you want within the boundaries of that vision.

What is the core of your long-term vision?

17 | Consider Your Vision's Impact

In his book *The Slight Edge*, Jeff Olson reveals that only 5% of people experience fulfillment by the end of their lives. If entrepreneurship were simple, you would see far more success stories far more consistently.

I have an exercise that will help you think through your semi-long-term aspirations and measure your commitment. You've considered what you want to accomplish decades from now, but I want you to think about your goals for the next three, five, and ten years. Remember that integrity requires you to commit to a clear plan. To achieve your "long-term" desires, you need to articulate your semi-long-term goals.

Take some time now to write down in 150 words or less where you want to be in 3 years, 5 years and 10 years. You can work through this exercise alone or call a few trusted people and ask them to help you explore your concept goals. Feel free to take a few days to thoroughly define your intentions.

What future impact would you like to make?

18 | Label Your Long-Term Vision

Now that you've thought through your 3-year, 5-year, and 10-year goals, narrow those 450 words to the 3 to 5 most critical words to describe your vision, both for you and the public.

Think back to the example of the Ritz-Carlton Hotel. Their three critical words could be serving, ladies and gentlemen. Your words might relate to your concept directly, indirectly or metaphorically. Just keep them relevant to your big picture. You can use your semi-long-term goals as a guide, but don't limit yourself.

These words should represent the overall culture of your venture, the stuff that will remain the same in spite of any obstacles. These words are the ones that should hold your venture together during trying times, forming your true north when all other points of reference go awry.

Once you've developed your list, join forces with mentors, potential business partners, or anyone else who can help you shape your vision. With this trusted group, narrow your list to the 3 to 5 words that best represent your true north. With this shortened list, you're on your way to developing your vision statement.

What 3 to 5 critical words define your vision?

19 | Define Your Long-Term Vision

Now that you've gained perspective on your future goals and the core importance of your venture, you're finally ready to write your vision statement.

Remember Leonardo da Vinci's observation: "Simplicity is the ultimate sophistication." Don't confuse your team. Don't confuse your client or customer either.

You'll want to be able to express your vision statement in a short, easy-to-put-on-a-t-shirt format.

You can begin by practicing different ways to audibly state your vision in ten seconds or less. Once again, start by making a list of 10 to 15 words that reflect your true north. This list might include your 3 to 5 most critical words. Don't take a lot of time on your initial list.

Next, think about action words that have lasting meaning for your concept. Once you've come up with your list of 10 to 15 action words, you'll once again need to narrow your list to your top 3 to 5. Don't hesitate to lean on the insight and wisdom of your support group for this exercise as well.

Great examples of practical vision statements include the following:

- The Ritz-Carlton —We are ladies and gentlemen serving ladies and gentlemen.

- Disney – We create happiness by providing the finest entertainment for people of all ages, everywhere.

- Human Rights' Campaign – Equality for everyone.

- Alzheimer's Association – Our vision is a world without Alzheimer's.

- Habitat for Humanity – A world where everyone has a place to live.

Strong statements will educate the public on your product or concept and will steady your company through disorienting times. Next we'll discuss how to form a winning mission statement

How would you communicate your vision in less than 20 words?

"**Strong** statements will **educate** the public on your product or concept

&

will **steady** your company **through** disorienting **times.**"

Step Four:
Shaping a Short-Term Mission

Step Four:
Shaping a Short-Term Mission

Your mission statement should reflect you, your employees, your brand and your culture. It should be action-oriented and express your goal for operating your business each day. How you address these aspects in your mission statement will contribute to your long-term success.

As your project grows, you'll need to understand that human nature tends to deviate from systems. Just showing up every day and expecting people to get with the program won't be enough. We all need frequent reminders to stick to our good intentions. This is why we live by calendars and day planners and why the project-management business is a multi-billion dollar industry. Thousands of people make a living by keeping thousands of other people on track.

This need rises partially from busyness but also from our habitual tendency to do what's comfortable for us. Delegated tasks, budgeted time and lists of responsibilities aren't comfortable. People cut corners and deviate from guidelines in sports, the classroom, their homes, work place and practically anywhere people participate. If you don't have a guiding statement that keeps you and everyone around you focused on the task at hand, you will deviate from the course. Your autopilot will automatically take over and at the end of every day, you'll notice the only things you accomplished were the things you wanted to do.

If you want a successful brand, however, you'll need to do things that stretch you out of your comfort zone. You'll need a guide to push you toward uncomfortable tasks. That guide is your mission statement.

In their book, *Strategic Management: An Integrated Approach*, Gareth Jones and Charles Hill state, "The mission statement should guide the actions of the organization, spell out its overall goal, provide a path, and guide decision-making. It provides 'the framework or context within which the company's strategies are formulated.'" The mission statement shares what the company hopes to achieve for society. By the end of this section, you should have some perspective on your brand's contribution to the world and will hopefully shape a statement that shares that desire.

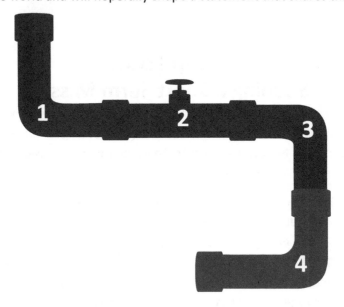

20 | Identify your Short-Term Goals

Your mission statement should state in no more than 15 words what your company sets out to accomplish. Unlike your vision statement, which is your distant point of reference, your mission statement focuses on the *now*. One of my favorite examples of a company with a great mission statement is TED (www.TED.com). Their statement is "spreading ideas," just a two-word statement reiterated daily to remind employees what their work is about.

Another example of a good mission statement comes from The Gifted Education Foundation (www.iamgifted.org), which describes the mission to "produce marketplace leaders from low-income communities across America." Though a bit longer than TED's, the statement remains simple enough to memorize and market but comprehensive enough to fully explain to the public and orient employees.

Just like you needed semi-long-term goals to determine your visionary end goal, you need current goals to achieve lasting success. When new ideas emerge, they'll tempt you to deviate from your plan, but you can stay on track with the guidance of a simple statement that gives you daily aim.

While you might feel overwhelmed by this task, I'll provide steps to help you create an effective mission statement. First, I recommend you work with a team that understands your mission. As we discussed in earlier chapters, you need to start by pinpointing the problem you're aiming to solve. Once you know the problem, you can sketch your solution on paper as a type of action formula where the actions add up to produce a solution. That formula becomes your mission statement.

What are you trying to accomplish short-term?

21 | Isolate the Problem

We'll begin with determining the problem you want to solve. People love to buy convenience. Hundreds of thousands of companies exist for the sole purpose of solving problems. You have to determine how your solution stands out among those working in the same space as you. Al "Bubba" Baker, former NFL athlete and founder of Bubba's Bar-B-Q & Catering Company, did just that when he patented a process for extracting bones from pork ribs.

Al's wife, who refuses to eat ribs with her hands, inspired his invention. When his wife rejected the messy dish, Al set out to find a way he could enjoy ribs with the woman of his dreams. With some research, he discovered lots of people shared a similar resistance as his wife. He pitched his idea on the popular TV show *The Shark Tank*, had a couple of sharks fight over the concept and hooked a contract with Daymond John, Founder of FUBU clothing company. Now his concept is exploding. Al Baker solved a problem of cleanliness and convenience. As a result, his target market, people who like BBQ ribs but hate the mess, responded on a wide scale.

You might know in your head the problem you want to solve, but you'll need to articulate it in a succinct statement. This will help you, your business partners, and your buyers understand and love your brand. Once again, I have a challenge in precision for you. Consider what makes your solution unique and think about how you can articulate it in 15 words or less. Consider hosting a think-tank gathering with like-minded leaders who can work with you on clarifying your niche and communicating your plan for impact. Once you've secured a stock of useful parts, you can begin shaping your mission statement. Aim to make it sticky enough that it's difficult to forget. Avoid statements so complex or overdone that people actually want to forget them.

Once you find a statement you're satisfied with, test it on some potential customers. Ask them for complete honesty, because when you brand your business with this statement, the public will respond with brutal honesty.

What problem are you trying to solve today?

22 | Clarify the Core of Your Short-Term Mission

Just like we did with your long-term vision, you'll need to uncover the core of your short-term mission. You need to honestly assess your motives for your current venture; otherwise your true motives will eventually influence your decisions and overpower your stated mission. Similarly, your motives will determine your company's culture. Because motives have so much influence, you should evaluate them and shape them intentionally; otherwise, your intentions and your actions will always oppose each other.

Simon Sinek, author of *Start with Why*, said almost everyone has the capacity to articulate what they do. Many people have the capacity to even articulate how they do it. Yet very few people have the clarity and the discipline to articulate why they do what they do. One of the greatest traps for a leader is to broadcast a mission statement that says one thing but moves toward another thing.

If your *why* is to simply make money, then target people who believe in pure capitalism, such as your investors, funders and long-term partners. If your why is about compassion and generosity, search out other philanthropists. You want to find those like-minded people because sooner or later you'll run into people whose values deviate from yours and you'll want the support of common minds.

While you search for people who share common goals with you, also remember that people with different values can offer helpful perspectives. You just want to make sure you choose people whose values remain relatively close to your own. The secret to successful partnerships is to stay honest and clear about your values so no one enters a business relationship disillusioned. Disillusionment can easily come across like dishonesty. If you've ever bought a product with high expectations only to be let down by a lack of quality, you know the suspicion and disgust that results from the let-down.

Know the central core of your mission and ensure that your mission statement says that clearly.

What is the core of your mission?

23 | Label Your Short-Term Mission

As with your vision statement, the only way to start on a mission statement is to begin writing. Start by placing a verb at the beginning of your statement that shows action toward a resolution. You can see this in TED's mission statement "spreading ideas." The first word states the action they're taking.

Once you've chosen the best action verb, the next step is to choose descriptors and nouns. The Gifted Education Foundation chose the action verb "produce," but the noun and descriptors reveal their full mission: "to produce marketplace leaders from low-income communities across America." The nouns, leaders and communities, define the benefactors of the cause while the three descriptors add more specifics. The organization doesn't just produce leaders; it produces *marketplace* leaders. And the leaders don't come from just anywhere; they come from *low-income communities across America.*

You'll need to think of a mission statement that speaks for your concept when you're not around. This means your statement needs to explain your concept and also defend it. In fact, by the end of your statement, the public should feel informed and somewhat committed to your brand.

Writing your mission statement is not a one-go step. It takes revision and often a lot of cutting (resist the urge to say it all in your mission statement). This process could take weeks or even months. With that in mind, do a lot of research and don't let the numerous rounds of editing discourage you. Take your time and seek the wisdom of trusted friends or potential partners, clients, and consumers.

What are the 3 to 5 most critical words that define your mission?

24 | Consider Your Mission's Future Impact

One way to begin nailing down the perfect mission statement is to describe the world or market and how it will change because of you. Consider how your concept can impact lives, efficiency, quality, and overall satisfaction. Clear perspective on how you want to change your environment can contribute to improving your civic impact as well as your profit sharing leverage, market capitalization and/or brand recognition.

Starbucks offers a great example of a company that was clear about the difference they wanted to make. Howard Schulz, founder and original CEO of Starbucks, decided years ago that he wanted to make Starbucks the "third place" for consumers. He wanted a brand so inviting that consumers would choose the Starbucks cafe as their hang out when away from home and work. Now, almost everyone has used Starbucks' free internet and comfortable couches to hold meetings, work independently or just relax. The leadership at Starbucks decided they didn't want to simply sell coffee. They wanted to sell an experience. That's exactly what they've done. They transformed the coffee industry by making coffee sales a by-product of their actual mission. Their coffee isn't necessarily any better than the other brands, but they sell their customers on the idea that Starbucks is their third home. With this mission, they lead at the front of the caravan of coffee brands.

Take some time now to think through your approach. What do you want to accomplish? How will you stand apart from others in the same industry? If your goal is to sell drills, don't just aim to sell drills. Aim to sell the most efficient process for creating a hole that money can buy. If your goal is to sell ice cream, don't just sell ice cream. Sell frozen joy. If you can get people to connect with the meaning behind your company's existence, you have a greater chance of gaining customer loyalty. The Gifted Education Foundation doesn't just give students a way out of poverty. They give hope and raise skilled, ethical workers who will go on to lead in Fortune 500 Companies, small businesses, non-profits and many other enterprises.

Determine now how your brand will make a unique difference in their lives.

How will the world be different because of your venture?

25 | Consider Your Mission's Present Impact

As you consider the future impact you want to make, think specifically how you want to impact the world on a daily basis. Blake Mycoskie, Chief Shoe Giver of TOMS Shoes, experienced a life-changing encounter while vacationing in Argentina in 2006. In his article for the *Business Insider*, he described his experience:

> I witnessed the intense pockets of poverty just outside of the bus-
> tling capital. It dramatically heightened my awareness. Yes, I knew
> somewhere in the back of my mind that poor children around the
> world often went barefoot, but now, for the first time, I saw the
> real effects of being shoeless: the blisters, the sores, the infections.

Blake's encounter inspired him to launch Shoes for a Better Tomorrow, what we know today as TOMS. The for-profit company provides a pair of shoes to a disadvantaged child each time someone purchases a pair of TOMS. Records show that at the end of 2013, TOMS had donated more than 10 million shoes to disadvantaged children. In addition to shoes, the company now sells eyeglasses to provide sight-saving medical services, and in 2014 Blake announced their team would move into the coffee business. With every bag of coffee purchased in a supplying country, the company will donate a week's worth of clean water to communities in need. All this manifested because Blake saw clearly the daily change he wanted to make.

While Blake's story represents an exceptional success, you too can have a lasting impact on the world. You have the same power to revolutionize an industry or even create a new one, but first you have to know the daily impact you want to make, how you hope to benefit your market. Keep in mind that, like TOMS, you might serve a direct market on a daily basis in order to serve an indirect market in the end. Be creative. Be innovative. Be daring. Be solutions-oriented. There's a reason you've locked onto this concept. Now you have to identify and define that reason.

What is the present impact of your venture?

26 | Describe Your Mission in 10 Seconds or Less

Use your imagination for a moment. Pretend you just entered an elevator from the first floor of a city tower and pressed the button to go to the 20th floor. On your way up, the elevator stops at the 10th floor. Coincidentally, your business hero happens to board the elevator, also heading to the 20th floor. In the brief time you have to ride from the 10th floor to the 20th floor, you have a unique opportunity to share your company's mission. Let's imagine further that at this moment your business hero turns to you and says, "You look very familiar to me. Do I know you from somewhere? What exactly do you do for a living?"

Your business idol just invited you to deliver one of the most important pitches you could ever give. Before you know it, your blood pressure begins to race, your heart starts to pound, your palms begin to sweat and ... well, the elevator ride ends. As soon as the elevator doors open, you and your hero part ways. You walk away disappointed, wondering how you could have allowed such a failed encounter.

While the story is a bit exaggerated, it attests to the importance of knowing your mission. In our imaginary scene, you missed what could have been a life-changing event because you never formulated a simple, easily-deliverable mission statement which you could give quickly while under pressure. You want to know your mission well enough that you can present it to anyone who approaches you with a brief window of time.

Many people falsely believe that long responses make them sound more intelligent, but brevity is our friend in such situations. You want to enlist your audience's support not dumbfound them with useless complexity. Meandering chatter will convince investors you lack clarity and persuasive leverage and are not worth the investment.

Don't let our elevator scenario happen to you. Take the time to consider how you would respond before you have to. A good length to shoot for is under ten seconds. Make it brief and keep it simple.

How would you describe your mission in 10 seconds or less?

27 | Define Your Short-Term Mission in 20 Words or Less

Like you did for your vision statement, writing short, simple, easy-to-put-on-a-t-shirt statements can help you hone in on your mission. Start with a list of 10 to 15 words that describe your main aims.

Remember this might look different from your vision. Your vision is your destination, while your mission is the avenue you take to get to that destination. As before, don't over-think your first draft. Use action verbs and specific nouns that tell who you serve. Keep your target customer or client in mind throughout this process and think about what words would describe for them the benefits you want to give them.

Once you've come up with your list of 10 to 15 words, you'll need to narrow your list to your top 3 to 5 words. Once you have a narrow list of action verbs and specific nouns, try arranging these words into a concise but descriptive mission statement.

Some good examples of mission statements include the following:

- **Facebook:** To give people the power to share and make the world more open and connected.

- **Google:** To organize the world's information and make it universally accessible and useful.

- **YouTube:** To provide fast and easy video access and the ability to share videos frequently.

- **Skype:** To be the fabric of real-time communication on the web.

- **Dell:** To be the most successful computer company in the world at delivering the best customer experience in markets we serve.

Your mission statement works together with your vision statement to lead you and your team in the right direction. Everyone involved with a mission has a personal responsibility to that mission, and your statements give the roadmap and destination for them to follow.

How would you write your mission statement in less than 20 words?

MISSION

"your *mission*

is the **avenue**

you take to get to that

destination."

destination

Step Five:
Developing a Strategy

Step Five:
Developing a Strategy

Now that you've clarified your concept and developed a healthy perspective on what you want to accomplish today (mission) and tomorrow (vision), you can begin focusing on your process for achieving those results. Now, you can begin creating a strategy.

Before you begin, however, make a deal with yourself that you won't let perfection get in the way of progress. Don't spend so much time developing a strategy that you miss your window of opportunity to launch your concept. Thousands of ideas go to the grave because the developers freeze at this step. Analysis paralysis arrests entrepreneurs every day and they never get anywhere as a result. Whatever you do, don't sit back and do nothing.

On the flipside, don't take off running without having some idea of the direction you want to go. Busy doesn't automatically equal productive. Make sure your actions add value to your venture.

To ensure your actions produce the desired results, begin developing a strategy. The previous creative steps might have been fun for you. Many people find their creative side easier to embrace because inspiration comes pretty effortlessly. While inspiration is great, perspiration is even more important. You've reached the pivotal point. Now, decide how you'll put action behind those ideas. Don't just think—do!

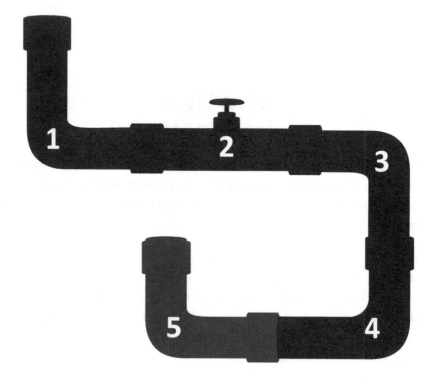

28 | Specify Your Audience

The first step to strategizing is to determine your primary customer. This can be difficult because you'll naturally want everyone to believe in your concept. Although you might feel this, you shouldn't let these feelings drive your actions. Examine your motives, maybe with the help of some trusted friends. If you aim to please everyone, you'll end up pleasing no one.

To drive this point home, I'd like to share my personal experience with choosing a manageable target market. Prior to launching The Gifted Education Foundation, I spent years mentoring low-income students. My wife and I invested thousands of hours and thousands of dollars in young people we believed had promising futures but who lacked critical support.

Soon, the two of us became overwhelmed by the hundreds of thousands of young people who needed support. It was then that I decided to take what I was doing individually and create a path for people all over the world to engage in similar work. People all over the world: that was my over-ambitious and overly general-ized goal in the brainstorming phase. But when we launched, we had defined our market as people who recognize the value of education and life skills in students trying to escape poverty. We were not and are not attempting to reach everyone on the planet.

Our defined audience allows us to accept the many negative responses we get. We get rejections, but we don't become discouraged because we realize these individuals aren't part of our market. If our market were still people everywhere, we might question our cause when we encounter rejection.

When people reject your idea, don't take it personally and don't let it deplete your confidence in your idea. Let people have their own preferences and recognize that they simply aren't your audience.

You'll need to think long and hard about the demographic you want to serve. When you focus on a specific group, word will spread and the right people will find you through good marketing and word of mouth. For The Gifted Education Foundation, our demographic was students in low-income communities throughout the United States. Once we narrowed our reach, other supporters of students from low-income communities came and continue to come to us. We keep on refining our methods, but our segmented market has inspired other supporters to link up with us.

Now, it's your turn to figure out the best way to reach your target demographic. Be very clear and unapologetic about the identity of your true audience. Limiting factors might include age, gender, economic status or occupation. Create a list of requirements, narrow your focus and commit!

Who are you targeting?

29 | Know Your Audience

Once you know *who* you want to reach, you'll need to learn more about them. Don't assume and don't generalize. You'll need to research your market to earn their respect and learn their tendencies. Make sure you're offering something your public wants. Just because you solve a problem for yourself doesn't mean everyone in your demographic has that problem.

A few years ago, Chick-fil-A announced, what I assumed to be, one of the greatest recipes known to mankind: The Coffee Caramel Milkshake. When it first came out, not a week went by that I didn't stop to pick one up. And then one day, I pulled up at the drive-thru window to request my frozen treat only to discover it was suddenly no longer offered. My heart was broken! I literally felt like it was the end of the world. Okay, not literally, but it was a fairly devastating day. That experience reminded me that my personal preferences don't always match the rest of the world's preferences.

Unfortunately, many business leaders lack this discipline. One of my mentors recently reminded me of something that sounds simple yet trips up many new entrepreneurs. A prototype should never be overvalued. Don't confuse prototypes with final products, no matter how much confidence you have in the design. Don't let your personal appreciation blind you from a concept's true readiness. Your job is to please your market, so let a market sample decide if your concept is ready for mass advertisement.

What do you know about who you're targeting?

30 | Know What the Audience Values

While on your journey to clarify who might invest in your venture, you'll also want to consider how much they'll invest. I recall a story about a church and its community development corporation that stumbled into an opportunity to take over a vacant restaurant. For years, the restaurant thrived as a mid-tier American diner that brought in approximately $20 per person. Eventually, though, the population shifted from middle-income families to low-income families, and the restaurant lost its high-paying customers.

The church planned to revitalize the community by reopening this restaurant as an independently operated dining option at the same dollar value as the previous restaurant. The problem lay in the new demographic. If residents purchased a fried chicken meal, they preferred to purchase it from KFC or Popeye's for 75% less than the fried chicken meal at this restaurant. Needless to say, the restaurant didn't survive. In hindsight, they realized they opened prior to surveying the market's potential value.

The same rule applies to you. One reason 90% of businesses fail within their first 3 years is that their designers don't assess their product's worth from their market's perspective. You've studied your market, now study your concept and imagine how they'll value it.

What is it worth to them?

31   Strategize Your Plan

It's time for you to think seriously about how you intend to accomplish your mission and vision. Many people know what they want to accomplish, but few take the time to plan _how_ they'll accomplish it.

Your execution plan for your mission and vision will form your strategy. In his book _Good Strategy, Bad Strategy: The Difference and Why It Matters_, Dr. Richard Rumelt describes strategy as a type of problem solving. He teaches that good strategy has an underlying structure called a _kernel_. The kernel has three parts:

1.   A _diagnosis_ that defines or explains the nature of the challenge

2.   A _guiding policy_ for dealing with the challenge

3.   Coherent _actions_ designed to carry out the guiding policy

For example, your _diagnosis_ might be to satisfy hungry customers. A component of your _guiding policy_ for dealing with the diagnosis is to produce food at a low cost and a rapid rate. Finally, a coherent _action_ to execute the guiding policy is to have the quickest service of any fast food restaurant while serving customers at a drive-thru window.

Now, think about your concept in the same framework. The nature of your concept likely comes from a need you see in the marketplace. This is your *diagnosis*. Next, think through your *guiding policies* for dealing with the challenge(s). To identify these, think about the three to five operating principles you consider necessary for your business or organization. Finally, once you clarify these, identify the *action* steps needed to execute these principles.

How are you going to accomplish your mission and vision?

32 | Deliver Your Product or Service

Whether you manufacture candles, bake cakes, provide strategic planning services, or run a community development corporation, you need an efficient and effective way to deliver your resource to your customers, clients, or beneficiaries.

The Gifted Education Foundation uses a four-phased strategy to support low-income students. The four phases are not inextricably linked, yet they work somewhat interdependently. Ideally, a student discovers our foundation in the 9th grade and receives our support through high school, college and even after they enter the workforce. However, some students leave the program in the 11th grade when they complete the Gifted Preparatory School (Phase 1). Other students with enough talent can bypass the Gifted Preparatory School and enter straight into the foundation's Gifted College Access Program (Phase 2). (To learn more about The Gifted Education Foundation strategy, check out the website at www.iamgifted.org). This model demonstrates the value of a structured process that helps you govern the delivery of your product or service.

The structured model provides a formula for how you choose to solve your focal problems. As you move forward, examine some of your competitors and learn their delivery models. Understand the pros and cons of their models so you can create a better delivery method. You should also study three to five successful business models that have nothing to do with your market. For example, you might examine the attributes of the best airline company or the finest dining experience. In his book *Good to Great,* Jim Collins offers tremendous insight into how *great* companies became the best companies in the world. I recommend you read that book and learn from the model companies Collins discusses.

One last bit of advice on this subject: don't underestimate the usefulness of examples of failure. Consider what weakness doomed Blockbuster when Netflix and Redbox hit the market. Other comparative models of failure include Kmart when compared with Wal-Mart, Circuit City versus Best Buy and the entire bookstore industry against Amazon. A great book to use when thinking about examples of failure is *How the Mighty Fall,* also written by Jim Collins. Wherever you choose to look for delivery examples, make sure you take the time to thoroughly examine the best strategic delivery model for your venture.

What process of delivery will you use?

33 | Format Your Venture

Before you begin developing your venture, you'll need to decide on the best angle for your approach. For example, if you're a committee chairperson of a local church that has decided to organize a 5K run/walk to save whales, you're operating a single project, not a full-blown business. A few years back, my son's elementary school discovered they weren't engaging enough fathers, so they called a few dads willing to take on the daunting task of pulling more men away from work to volunteer at school. In this example, we would define their angle as a community project. Each type of activity requires a different approach for defining, designing, and delivering.

You have to recognize the difference between the various approaches and know the best direction for your situation. This will help everyone involved understand the underlying objective and the means to that desired end. For example, you don't want your people wasting time to set up a 501c3 for a non-profit when you're really developing a community project that will have a completion term.

Know your objective first. Then, begin building an infrastructure to support it. Talk to others. Get wisdom. Don't think and operate in isolation. Take the time to select the best format that will bring you to your objective. Then go for it!

What is the best format for your venture?

34 | Map the Best Location for Your Venture

As you approach kick-off day for your venture, you'll need to consider the best place to set up your operation. If, for example, you're a single mother hoping to create a cosmetics supply company, your operation might thrive best in your garage or home. If you're also caring for a home and family, you might not have the luxury to leave your current full-time job and head to an after-hours office away from home. On the other hand, you might be married with kids and living in a house that has little to no space for inventing. In this case, you won't want to set up shop in your home because your daily family operations could interfere with your business. In such a situation, a small operation in a rented space outside the home would probably suit you better. Don't rush through this step carelessly. Location constraints can destroy young entrepreneurs before they even gain momentum.

A friend of mine decided he wanted to become a motivational speaker with a concentration in the corporate Fortune 500 market. He knew that in order to build bridges with the influential members of this community he had to spend time in locations where he had access to decision makers. So he and his wife uprooted from their home of ten years and set up shop in Minneapolis, MN. Along with this move, he sacrificed a lucrative corporate position as the vice president of one of the most highly recognized hotel brands in the world. Ultimately, his dream was only possible because he was willing to take an honest look at the circumstances and make the move to the necessary setting.

Just as my friend had to make sacrifices to give his venture the optimum environment, you might have to deal with some discomfort for the sake of ideal real estate. This might mean you have to free up a room in your home, invest in a small office space, request that someone partner with you and allow you to share some of their extra space, or even relocate completely. Whatever your situation, make sure you've set yourself up for success and, if you haven't, be open to change.

Where should you locate your venture's operations?

35 | Set Development Stages

When I established The Gifted Education Foundation, I knew I had to begin by surrounding myself with people smarter than me. Our founding board members ranged from a retired CEO of a Fortune 200 Company to Ivy-League-educated executives from corporate, non-profit and conventional academic settings. I formed a broad community because I knew that no matter how much I planned or how much corporate and non-profit experience I had, I would face unfamiliar obstacles. I needed people who had different skills and perspectives to challenge me to slow down, speed up or reconnect with reality as needed.

I looked to organize a group of the most talented leaders I could find, met with them one-on-one and absorbed their advice. After gathering all the notes and feedback I received from my meetings, I concluded that the best thing for me to do was roll our model out slowly to capture tangible data. This data would include statistics like the number of college applicants, scholarships applied for, and scholarships received. We needed this information to assess the needs of the schools and families.

It took a lot of discipline to resist my desire to go big and go big immediately, but I've seen many cases where bigger and faster destroyed organizations. The downside of rushing into growth outweighs the frustration of slow accuracy. Are there anomalies? Absolutely! Are you the next anomaly? Possibly. Should you plan like you're NOT the next anomaly? Yes.

Expect the absolute best scenario, but prepare for the absolute worst scenario. Leaders who assume everything will go exactly as planned are doomed. In my case, our foundation made plans but took time to survey the audience instead of entering the market thinking we had everything figured out. As we learned about our audience, our plans changed and we added elements and removed others.

No matter how confident you feel, take some time to learn the demands of your market and surround yourself with people who have different wisdom to offer. When you've formed a band of trusted mentors, heed their advice. You don't have to implement all their recommendations, but you should take advantage of their wisdom while planning your development stages. With these informed development stages you'll still experience obstacles, but you'll get past them.

What are your development stages?

36 | Identify Your Cyclical Revolutions for Success

Many of the most successful entrepreneurs are successful because they take time to project, plan, execute and examine their business models. Over the years, I've experienced many scenarios where leaders govern their organizations or businesses with a reactive mindset instead of a proactive one. They only react to the demands that surround them, making decisions based upon knee-jerk reactions instead of planning ahead and setting up systems to manage future problems.

People create businesses, but systems sustain them. Whether you're just beginning or running a 20-year old "institutionalized" organization, you have to learn from cyclical revolutions. To help you do this, let's walk through the four steps: *project, plan, execute, examine.*

Project

As you think about your product or service, think about the delivery cycles. What makes a cycle for your offering? For example, if you want to develop an independent middle school for girls, you're cycle would be a school year, so you would need to consider what you need to make it through that cycle. You would need to project how much you need in capital, staff positions, textbooks, and equipment. You'd also have to plan for how advanced the technology in the school will be and how much involvement you'll ask from your community partners. You can't predict everything accurately, but you can develop reasonable projections. You'll probably find that you end up closer to your projections than you anticipated. Although they're not perfect, projections help you create a successful business model.

Plan

Proverbs 15:22 (NIV) states, "Plans fail for lack of counsel, but with many advisers they succeed." Once you've nailed down your list of projections, the next step in considering cyclical revolutions is to develop a cyclical strategy. Your business as a whole needs to have an operating strategy as discussed previously. However, this cyclical strategy specifically aims at your product or service line strategy. Using the middle school example again, after projecting the number of staff needed, you would put a talent acquisition plan in place. This plan might include developing job descriptions, detailing criteria for certification or checking out different social media outlets for recruitment. You should strategize for every component that contributes to the success of your revolution cycle.

Execute

It's all about execution! Stan Epperson, a colleague and member of my board, asked me a profound question: "Anthony, if you were to get twenty Fortune 500 CEOs together for a brainstorming session and capture their ideas for an entire day, how much do you think that brainstorming session would be worth?" Of course, my initial reaction was to say, "Wow! Stan, I couldn't even imagine what that would be worth!" How amazing would it be to have some of the best and brightest minds in the same room to share their perspectives on innovations that could revolutionize the world? But then he chuckled and answered his own question: "Anthony, those ideas pulled together in the nicest, leather bound portfolio you can imagine would be worth every bit of ten bucks!" Why? Because it's the execution that counts, not just the ideas.

The same applies to you as you think about the cyclical revolutions of your product or service. Jordan Martin introduced the drive-thru window in the United States in the 1930s. He wanted customers to feel free to remain in their vehicles when purchasing food. The concept has flourished and spread to a number of sectors including banking, ice cream, cleaners, post offices, libraries, pharmacies, coffee shops, and even churches! Yes, there really are churches that have morning and evening options available for people to drive by, share their concerns and receive prayer without ever leaving the comfort of their vehicle. Some statistics show that McDonald's and many other recognized brands in the fast food industry have earned as much as 50% of their profits as a result of the drive-thru. The idea was to sell convenience, and it was a winning concept, but projecting and planning wouldn't have changed the food industry. Execution made the difference.

Although execution is everything, you'll still need to make sure you first think through the revolutionary cycle of execution (e.g. how many burgers do you want to sell per hour) along with the systems, infrastructure, and people needed to do that effectively. If, however, you've projected and planned, go and execute, execute, execute!

Examine

Once you've developed a list of reasonable projections, created a plan for those projections, and executed that plan, you should then go back and examine the first three phases. Many business leaders randomly move through the first three components and move on without ever taking the time to examine whether their previous work was successful. In fact, many don't even define success or failure in the first place. If you don't know your target, anywhere you aim will suffice. Some people determine their success based on intuition, but I encourage you to exhaust as much energy in defining success as you do causing that success.

When you examine, you want to focus on anything that will help you better manage where you failed and replicate where you succeeded. Take the time to record as much detail as possible to substantiate what gets you to every phase in your venture's cycle. This is important for a number of reasons. For example, if you get hit by a bus, you want to know that your business or organization can continue to move forward without you. Detailed documentation will allow another individual to pick up where you left off.

Suppose you run a cleaning supply company. You've been operating as a mom-and-pop shop, managing a database of small clients gained through referrals, when an angel investor comes along and wants to partner with you to help you expand. This could provide you with financial stability, but first this investor wants to see some documents showing how you've managed your infrastructure up to this point. These documents would include financial records, reports from clients with varying levels of satisfaction, a log of potential clients and a scalability plan. You should always prepare for a situation like this. In addition to serving as evidence for investors, collecting data also helps you learn your business better so you can anticipate and prepare for snares.

Have no fear if you've slacked in this area. It's not too late. You can begin collecting data now. Be sure you take time to examine your track record and keep a database available for easy access as you continue to grow and expand your concept.

What are your cyclical revolutions for success?

37 | Identify Your Cyclical Evolutions for Success

There's a huge difference between revolutionary cycles and evolutionary cycles. Blockbuster Video, at the peak of the company's success, had more than 9,000 stores and more than 60,000 employees. It was by far the leading store in the industry, with an executive leadership team many other organizations envied. But, like many companies that grow to their size, they overlooked something. Every large company, including those that succeed like Blockbuster, has to make adjustments and maintain agility in their market. Their "revolutionary cycles" were not their Achilles' heel. Their inattention to "evolutionary cycles" is what made them vulnerable to destruction.

In Blockbuster's case, their product offering *revolved* but didn't *evolve*. In other words, they continued to crank out business on a daily basis using the same framework they always used: renting movies and hoping to make killer profits off the irresponsible customers' late fees. That was a great idea initially, but as the market continued to *evolve*, the concept steadily lost momentum. Who cares if you put all the energy in the world in projecting, planning, executing, and examining if it's the wrong product, wrong business model or wrong solution to the problem? You have to realize that one winning idea today might not always be a winning idea. You'll need to respond to the demands of a changing market if you want to sustain long-term. Netflix and Redbox brought the adaptability Blockbuster lacked to the marketplace and put the orthodox movie store chain out of business.

Reed Hastings, the founder of Netflix, confessed that his inspiration for his company came as a result of a $40 late fee for a single movie. Netflix capitalizes on their unique offerings, which allow customers immediate access to movies (even from their mobile devices) and frees them from inconvenient fees. If this wasn't enough, they provide unlimited viewings for less than $10 a month. Blockbuster chose stagnation, and as a result, they folded. In fact, in the early 2000s, Blockbuster had the opportunity to purchase Netflix for approximately $50 million. They passed. Blockbuster filed for bankruptcy, and Netflix currently has more than 40 million subscribers, earning more than $4.37 billion in revenues in 2013.

You want to have a secure framework in place for revolution (basic cyclical turns in your business model) but also leave room for evolution (elasticity and adaptability). Don't be the next Blockbuster Video.

What are your cyclical evolutions for success?

"**Expect** the absolute
BEST scenario

but

prepare for the absolute
WORST
scenario."

Step Six:
Penetrating the Market

Step Six:
Penetrating the Market

One of the simplest and most effective steps you can take is to go where your customers are. If you don't figure out an efficient and effective way to get your service or product to the people who want or need it, your entire mission will amount to nothing.

As a unique example, I can't tell you the number of times ministries and organizations have asked me to lead workshops to help them expand their capacity to reach young people in their community. Without fail, the groups I have spoken to have had a common issue: *they weren't going where young people hang out.* Of course, it takes much more than simply showing up to establish an effective and engaging relationship with students. But the first step to connecting with them is to be where they are.

I walked away from corporate in my early twenties after feeling compelled to become a student pastor at New Direction Christian Church (NDCC) in Memphis, TN. The first thing I did was visit schools in my community. I attended football and basketball games, spoke at practices, chaperoned lunch hours, tutored and held pizza parties, among many other things. I did everything I could to place myself where high school students hung out so I could share the *Good News*. I actually grew up in a city where there were more churches than gas stations and liquor stores combined, yet churches never sought me out. I knew that when I made my transition, in order to reach marginalized students that resembled me in my teenage years, I had to hang out where marginalized students like me actually hung out. NDCC had a lot of helpful assets, including a supportive and engaging senior pastor, willing volunteers, and a generous budget. Ultimately, though, none of those things would have mattered to the success of the mission if I hadn't taken the time to go where the students hung out.

Another reason you need to place yourself around your clients is to survey their needs. The Gifted Education Foundation is affiliated with a firm in Southern California called Bedrock Creek Investments. As a partner of this firm, one of our top priorities is to work with municipalities in order to support in tackling the large-scale issues many cities face. These issues include unsatisfactory education, homelessness and human sex trafficking among many others. Our team travels to communities where these issues run rampant for the purpose of working with investors, city leadership, public servants, NGOs, churches and residents, all to gain a greater appreciation for addressing these issues. Our research has led to pilot projects in several US cities. We have tested and proved our model. But, we started by immersing ourselves with people who needed what our ground team could deliver. In our second year of operating as a comprehensive entity, our firm secured more than $1,000,000 in contracts in a single, thirty-day period.

While the aforementioned examples are clearly unique and distinct from everyday business and industry, the principles are certainly transferable. Bottom Line: you have to go to the location of your potential buyers to test for demand. Identify the problem, survey the people, create a solution and then take your product to the people. The next four chapters will give you guidance on how to do just that.

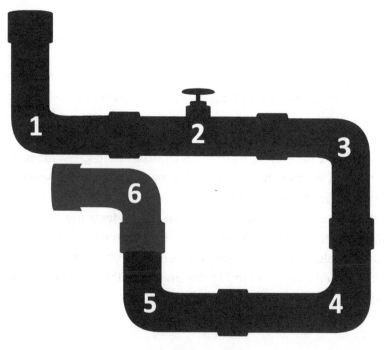

38 | Identify Your Zealots

I define a zealot as someone radical and relentless in beliefs or ideas. Your zealots will become your voices, your public relations arm, your branding team and much more.

Paul Edwards, the Executive Director of a billion-dollar campaign called the Wycliffe Bible Translators Languages Campaign, first worked for The GAP (clothing company) to identify their most loyal customers. Paul spent two years surveying stores and identifying customers who spent more than $1,000 in a single visit. Paul and his team defined those extreme loyalists as *zealots.* In his research, Paul discovered that the leading inspiration for those shoppers was the sight of young, smiling faces. Paul's findings led GAP Inc. to restructure their employment and hiring process. Their new standard became an energized retail environment primarily staffed with smiling teens that worked the registers and stocked the shelves. The GAP developed a business model that attracted more zealots because they endured a short-term re-staffing inconvenience that led to long-term gain.

Maybe you've had a zealot or two in your life. These are the people who believed in you when no one else would. Zealots can be parents, siblings, friends, a boyfriend or girlfriend, teachers, coaches, or anyone else who sees something in you with an unwavering tenacity.

Do everything possible to build an initial model that attracts zealots. Begin a dia-logue with your zealots now and bring them on board as quickly as possible, even in the prototype stages. This stage won't offend them. They want quality, but they'll journey with you as you build toward quality.

How will you identify your zealots?

39 | Strategize Your Customer Acquisition

A customer acquisition strategy will help you avoid marketing mistakes. Without it, you can make costly mistakes involving timing, location, medium, and price.

Startups run the risk of marketing their product, business, or organization prior to having a true value gauge. You only get one first impression. You want your product or service at its best when you launch, and you want just the right amount of customers to match your production capacity. A not-so-ready product could turn away users who might never give you a second chance. Not only will you waste capital to fix what's broken, you'll have to invest in promotional clean up. Relationships and reputation are both at stake. Protect both by timing your customer acquisition. Don't make your launch a practice run.

In addition to timing, quality and quantity, you'll need to measure your customer acquisition costs (CAC). To calculate this, first determine your expenses for manufacturing, production, marketing and distribution over a set period of time. Then divide this number by the number of customers who purchase your product or service. As an example and for simplicity purposes, let's assume your expenses for manufacturing, production, marketing and distribution for widget sales over a one-year period equate to approximately $1,000,000. Next, let's assume 5,000 customers purchased a widget from you within that one-year time frame. You would quantify your Customer Acquisition Costs as follows:

CAC = $1,000,000 over 12 months / 5,000 Customers = $200 per customer

When calculating your cost, consider your marketing options carefully so you don't invest unnecessary money on advertisements in places where people won't use your product. The goal is to reach the highest number of users at the lowest investment. For example, if you sell African-American hair care products, you might promote them on a hip-hop radio station. Just to be clear, not all African-Americans listen to hip-hop, but enough do that the station makes a worthwhile marketing investment. Consider the cheapest, most effective avenues you can take to reach your customers.

Let me give you an example of a wise customer acquisition strategy I recently witnessed. My son and I went to a shopping mall for lunch one day. As we headed for the food court, an employee of an Asian restaurant approached us with a piece of teriyaki chicken on a toothpick. As a result of this small sample, my son chose the Asian restaurant over the fifteen other options. The employee hooked us and we spent $20 in three minutes. If we assume that the total cost of rent, hourly salary for the employee, chicken, teriyaki sauce, and toothpick all combine for a total of one dollar during that three minute window, that makes a 20:1 return on investment. Their strategy was to find hungry customers, have them sample their food and bait shoppers into making a purchase. It worked with us and clearly with many others, as their business is still alive and thriving.

You'll need to devise your own strategy that gets you in front of as many potential customers as possible for as small an investment as possible. But be ready to deliver when they show up. Customer acquisition and product supply work together to form a successful business.

What is your customer acquisition strategy?

40 | Manage Your Suppliers

Often peoples' natural instinct tempts them to go with the cheapest supplier. However, if that supplier produces low quality, more harm than good could be done in the process.

If you're developing a business that requires you to buy products from other manufacturers, think strategically about how you'll manage your suppliers. First, you'll want to keep in mind that the best suppliers offer services that either match or exceed your expectations for quality, reliability, pricing, and partnership.

As a practice scenario, imagine you run a pie-baking business. You'd want to consider price, but even more importantly, you'd want to consider freshness. So when you choose your supplier, you'll need someone close enough and efficient enough to provide ingredients early in their shelf life. You'll also need someone who cares about the quality and purity of their products.

As you think about selecting suppliers, talk to competitors and investigate your options. In our example, you would target trade shows and associations and speak with grocery suppliers and business advisors. This is where relationships will help move your venture forward.

When developing relationships with suppliers, don't underestimate the importance of reciprocity. You can't expect suppliers to bend over backwards for you if you don't invest the same amount of time and energy into doing the same. Try your best to create a win-win scenario.

The suppliers you choose will influence your brand's reputation, so choose carefully. As much as possible, gather some different suppliers as options and evaluate which will work best for your needs.

How do you choose suppliers for your business?

41 | Structure the Business — Legally

Business structures are not one-size-fits-all. Specific structures suit specific ventures.

Before we get into how to structure a legal business, make sure you have an actual business in mind and not just a single product. Also consider whether you should sell or license your product rights to someone else. Remember the three types of people Bob Shank described: originators, organizers, and operators. Incredible product designers might lack the skills to start and sustain the actual organization or business. Make sure you have the skills and commitment before you jump into building your business structure.

If you do intend to move beyond a product and do want the responsibility of establishing a business, you have a few options. The most common option is used to target the elimination of personal and tax liabilities. These precautions can save you from high taxes, administrative and time depletion, personal asset destruction and many other issues. If you want more information on the types of legal structures available to you, explore a local library, visit a small business association, or talk to people who have started the type of business you're considering.

If you don't know what type of business you should pursue, browse the descriptions below.

- Sole Proprietorship – An individual or couple runs the business. This is the most common type of business because it's easy to operate and allows flexibility for taxes, management, and legal control.

- General Partnership – Two or more people agree to contribute labor, time, skill, and money equally. Each person shares the responsibility of the profits, losses, debts, liabilities, and management tasks.

- Limited Liability Partnership – Similar to the general partnership but no one partner takes on the liabilities of another partner in the business. Each partner accepts the consequences of his or her own actions.

- <u>Corporation</u> – A group of equal partners run the business. This structure has financial and tax benefits but also additional burdens, such as licensing fees and regulations.

- <u>Non-Profit Corporation</u> – A corporation that works to further an idea or achieve a goal besides pure profit. Most of these structures serve public interest, but *corporate foundations* are non-profits that work in the private sector.

The business structure you choose will shape your company's work environment and sometimes the public's view of you. It also determines the type of income tax form(s) you'll need to file each year. Consider your options and choose the right model to gives your vision the best chance.

How should you legally structure the business?

"devise your **own strategy** that gets you in front of as MANY **potential** CUSTOMERS as possible for as **small** an **investment** as possible."

Step Seven:
Defining Your Success

Step Seven:
Defining Success

If you don't have a clue what you're aiming for then any target will do. Many people claim they want *success* but fail to quantify and qualify it. A common barrier to completing your mission is often a failure to define success.

Let's say you have a goal to lose weight. Unless you set markers for success, you probably won't succeed and you certainly won't know when you've lost weight if you're not quantifying it. To know if you have succeeded, you need to mark goals for exercise, food and drink intake and lifestyle. Well, the same rule applies to your venture. You have to sit down and define success, both the major and the minor wins.

Dr. Gail Matthews, a psychology professor at Dominican University in California, did a goal-setting study involving 267 students. Her research showed that people are 42% more likely to achieve their goals when they write them down. By writing down your intentions, you give them clarity and priority.

When I was in high school, I had a crush on a girl. I had a single conversation with her, went home, called my best friend, and said, "Dude, I am going to marry that girl!" That girl and I (at the time of writing this book) are now going on nineteen years of living our dreams together, happily married with two amazing children. I captured my intentions for family along with plans to earn a full-scholarship to play football in college, to become a successful businessman, work for a major corporation, become a CEO and many other goals. With God's grace, I've accomplished the vast majority of the things I wrote down in high school. And, the journey isn't over yet!

Take a moment to define your own success so you can put yourself in the best position to hit your intended target. If you don't know your aim, you'll accept any target, even the wrong one.

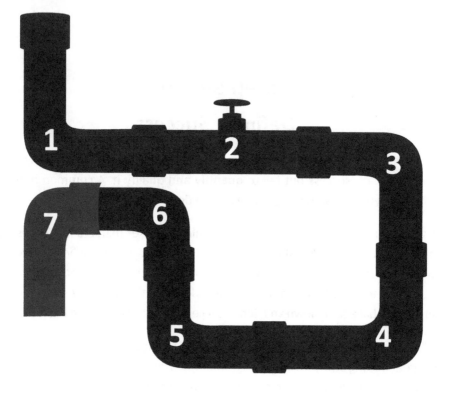

42 | Define Your Idea of Success

As you begin defining success, start by outlining categories where you want to see achievement come to life. For example, maybe you want to take an idea you have for a tech company, share it with a group of investors, secure capital for startup, launch a company, take it public and exit with a massive amount of wealth. You should write each of these steps down as a success marker.

Maybe you hope to go to college, land an internship with a major corporation, study abroad for a year or two, get an advanced degree, work in corporate America, move into management and eventually start your own company. When you define your wins, strategize to reach those goals and execute that strategy, you increase your likelihood of success.

I didn't prioritize financial wealth. I valued human impact and felt most inspired when I used my ability to influence and empower others. Therefore, I walked away from corporate America in my early twenties, where I managed a three-state territory with 3M (a Fortune 100 giant). I set a new goal to lead a well-recognized, non-profit organization on a national platform. I desired an influential organization with leadership that people all over the world would benchmark. I was able to accomplish that in my late twenties for a number of reasons. First, I defined success. Second, I found leaders and mentors who believed in me. And third, I chased knowledge. I have literally read hundreds of books, been to various types of trainings, obtained a Master's degree, received numerous certifications, placed myself around people who were ten times more accomplished than me, and invested in authentic relationships with people who could challenge and inspire me. Now my dream is emerging. An infrastructure that will outlive me will lead thousands of young people through college, career and life skills development. I defined success and now I'm seeing the fruit of my intentions.

You'll need to define the success you desire. Avoid letting others define it for you. Your friends and mentors should help you shape and inspire your definition, but they should never have full authority to define it for you. I know so many people who have made everyone around them happy but let personal happiness escape because they've allowed others to define their success. The exception would be if you're working as a team. In this case, you all want to define success together. You might even hire someone to facilitate a group dialogue. If you plan to lead your venture on your own, however, you should think about what success means to you.

What types of success are important to you?

43 | Define Your Idea of *Good*

Think about what *good* looks like for the next several years. *Good* can mean achieving your standards of success, but what if your standards don't require your full effort. *Good* goals should stretch you and challenge you to expand your business model.

Take a moment to paint a picture of what *good* accomplishments will look like for you in one, three and five years. Don't worry about the specifics yet. For now, reserve the list for big picture accomplishments. Your list could look something like this:

One-Year Accomplishments:

- Business or Non-Profit: Complete a comprehensive analysis of the Execution Pipeline

- Business: Raise X in start-up capital
- Business or Non-Profit: Develop a 3-Year strategic plan
- Business or Non-Profit: Develop a 3-Year budget and financial projections
- Business: Develop a customer survey tool

Three-Year Accomplishments:

- Business or Non-Profit: Survive the "3-year death cycle"
- Business or Non-Profit: Develop a 5-year growth plan
- Business or Non-Profit: Operate at 80% of revenues generated
- Business or Non-Profit: Have complete clarity around board needs and have every seat filled
- Business or Non-Profit: Have a state-of-the-art Annual Report in place

Five-Year Accomplishments:

- Business: Create profit margins 5% above industry standards
- Business: Have a proven track record for increasing gross sales by 10% annually on average
- Business or Non-Profit: Be recognized as a "best-in-class" entity
- Non-Profit: Have a minimum of 25 Community Partner agreements in place
- Business or Non-Profit: Be sufficiently staffed for scale while maintaining a financial surplus

Make sure your list suits your needs and only includes goals you can obtain. You'll do this by keeping true to your definition of success and not focusing on your competitors' definition of success. You can benchmark yourself against other competitors but don't exhaust yourself trying to be the very best version of someone else. Be the very best version of you!

What does good look like in 1, 3 or 5 years?

44 | Define Your Idea of Great

Great goals should stretch you to reach beyond your limits. Don't set such unreasonable intentions that you doom yourself. However, you do want to stretch yourself to the point where you'll need a significant amount of influence and resources beyond what you currently have in place. Someone once told me you should "dream of something so big that unless God is in it, it is doomed to failure." The following are some examples of difficult yet doable goals:

One-Year Accomplishments:

- Business: Have a product launch that consumes 1% of total market share

- Business: Experience 50% margins in gross profit after a year of operation

- Non-Profit: Raise enough capital to end the first year of operations with 25% cash on hand

- Business: Be featured in a major publication as one of the Top 10 Companies on the Rise

- Business: Have $1 million in gross sales

Three-Year Accomplishments:

- Business or Non-Profit: Gain recognition as a leader in the industry or sector on a local or regional level

- Non-Profit: See a 100% increase in membership from the previous year

- Business: Sell business for a 3 times multiple of gross sales

- Business: Become a supplier for the largest retail chain in the industry

- Non-Profit: Secure a large federal grant for regional community and economic development

Five-Year Accomplishments:

- Non-Profit: Secure a three year, federally funded grant at a seven-figure value

- Business: Sell business for a 5 times multiple of gross sales for year 3

- Business: Exceed a valuation of $1 Billion

- Non-Profit: Scale to 5 cities with a fully operational and funded model

- Non-Profit: Develop both a "best-in-class" regional, national, and international presence with full-scale operations in place and funded

Again, *great* goals should stretch you but not break you. Approach these with courage and tenacity but don't confuse foolishness for faith.

What does great *look like in 1, 3 or 5 years?*

45 | Define Your Smart Goals

As you design and plan your good and great goals, you also want to frame some key metrics for success along the way.

You should have at least three but no more than six key metrics. Having too few metrics won't challenge you enough, but too many tempts you to do mediocre work. These numbers come from my personal experience in helping people set goals and define metrics for success. Whether three or six is your number, the point is that you should push yourself to take action without overwhelming yourself and losing momentum.

As you begin to roll out your goals, assure they are S.M.A.R.T., a term originally coined by George Doran in a paper he wrote in the November 1981 issue of the *Management Review*. The mnemonic acronym stands for the following:

- Specific – clearly articulated

- Measurable – quantifiable e.g. %, $, #

- Assignable – able to be delegated to a specific person/team

- Realistic – can be achieved with the available resources

- Time-Related – has a determined completion date

People who exhibit S.M.A.R.T. goals and stick to them have a higher likelihood of success. Be sure you develop S.M.A.R.T. goals and allow these goals to dictate your day-to-day actions toward living out the success of your venture.

How will you define your S.M.A.R.T. goals?

46 | Consider Contradictions to Your Success

Failure is inevitable. For some it's drastic, for others it's minimal. Either way, it's inevitable. Many concepts, organizations and businesses fail because they don't anticipate failures and what causes those failures.

Failure sometimes emerges because of a more deeply rooted problem. You have to acknowledge your potential for failure just as much as you acknowledge your potential for success. While no formula for predicting challenges and failures is perfect, you can anticipate some potential barriers to success. I challenge you to think about some of these long-term contradictions to success and sustainability. The goal is not for you to feel intimidated; the goal is for you to prepare as much as possible.

I encourage you to take a look at case studies, specifically those of companies that led their industries and then suddenly died. When I was in college, I interned with Standard Register, a Fortune 500 company and leader in the paper-supply indus-try. Unfortunately, this company didn't find a way to pivot in response to a major technology shift and a paperless society. The leadership team didn't respond to market demands, and as a result, they ended up shutting their doors. I watched our entire sales force evaporate.

Do everything possible to protect your venture from a similar end. I assure you, many people believe such a tragedy could never happen to them, yet it happens to about 90% of them. Statistics suggest that 90% of businesses fail within their first three years of operations. When this is the case, don't be so foolish to believe you're exempt. Remember to expect the best, but plan for the worst.

What are some underlying contradictions to success?

47 | Identify Your Personal Obstacles

A lot of factors will weigh against you in your venture, and the odds of failure out-number the odds of success. You should not, however, set off with a doomed-to-fail mentality. You should instead prepare to work through typical start-up challenges.

Some of the challenges you'll face will result because of personal limitations. One of my favorite books is *Courageous Leadership* by Bill Hybels, Founding Pastor at Willow Creek Church in Chicago. In the book, Bill gives three important elements for assessing people in the workplace: competency, character, and chemistry. While his theory is for examining potential employees, you can also use it to examine yourself from the perspective of the person sitting across the table from you.

The first personal problem you might encounter is the competency barrier. For example, let's say you have an incredible idea that would enable you to influence the healthcare industry by making quality healthcare more affordable in third world countries. Suppose your concept requires you to erect facilities, identify a capable team to lead in a politically challenging setting, and raise the necessary capital to execute the concept. In this situation, you might face limitations such as a lack of business experience or minimal resources for construction and land development. You might have a good idea, but if you lack the tools or knowledge, the project might not be practical. We call these challenges competency barriers.

The second type of personal barrier deals with character weaknesses. Suppose you have the skills necessary to build one of the largest, most successful wealth management firms, but you have a track record of impropriety in your work. The temptation to behave the same way will always exist, even if you fight it. Just working in the industry and seeing others around you face the same struggles will remind you of your own fight. You'll need to determine whether you've developed enough willpower to resist those temptations. I know people who couldn't handle temptations in industries like real estate, financial management and even pastoral ministry. Don't allow your talent to take you where your character can't sustain you. Too many people have their lives disrupted and even destroyed because they overestimated the strength of their character.

Chemistry is the third pillar that could create personal barriers to your success. You could simply be unpleasant to be around. Business founders often battle with this because their positions give them power, prestige and privilege. Assess how well you interact with other customers, clients, employees, merchants, suppliers and anyone else you encounter in your venture. You could permanently burn a bridge, which might devastate your odds of success. Make sure you're developing the best *you* before you try to develop a great business. Don't slack off on your presentation of yourself. You need to continually improve your leadership skills, career skills, spiritual state, physical state and anything else your employees or market might judge.

Fight to keep your competency, character and chemistry calibrated. If you fall short in any of these areas for too long, you'll struggle to keep any idea alive. Check yourself before you wreck yourself. As a potential business grows and demands increase, the leader needs to match up to the growth. To do this, the leader needs the ability to guide supporters. A great book on this subject is *Derailed: Five Lessons Learned from Catastrophic Failures in Leadership* by Dr. Tim Irwin. It provides examples of leaders who held some of the most prominent positions known to mankind yet squandered them due to their inability to maintain one or more of the aforementioned qualities. Whatever you do, don't let *you* get in the way of success for your concept, business or organization.

What personal challenges could prevent you from succeeding?

48 | Identify Your General Obstacles

The 4th quarter of 2008 and the months – even years – that followed was one of the most difficult times the U.S. has faced. The economic downturn, arguably the worst since The Great Depression, led many people to lose jobs, businesses, homes and almost half their net worth. Regardless of their intelligence, connections, or wise money management, the crisis devastated millions of people. Instead of a reward for hard work, success became a game of luck. Many businesses, organizations, and ideas folded under the pressure, but thousands of other new concepts came to life in response to the challenges, and some pre-existing businesses actually benefitted from the crisis. Many fast food restaurants, for example, experienced a spike in sales as a result of people finding less expensive ways to dine and entertain their families. The lesson we can take away from that time is that no one is so intelligent that they can predict exact fluctuations of the economy.

Many factors influence the success of businesses, and many of them lie beyond the control of the people affected. While you can't predict all possible outcomes, you should consider the factors that could jeopardize your success.

During the economic crisis, I was serving as the Chief Operating Officer of a nationally renowned non-profit organization. I managed a multi-million-dollar budget, more than twenty staff members, and the delivery of programs and services in more than thirty U.S. cities. Unfortunately, the bulk of our funding came from generous individuals and family foundations that saw almost half their net worth evaporate within months. As the economy affected them, it also affected us. Despite our staff and budget cuts, we continued our services and faced the risks of trusting in what we called "new funders," who didn't yet exist. We dissolved programs and dismissed people who had helped build the brand. It was a painful task, but the cost of continuing the same pace in a changing economy far outweighed the costs of downsizing. We fell into a situation beyond our control, one that forced us to respond in a way we couldn't have predicted just a year earlier.

After much consideration, along with the counsel of supporters, we shaved our staff by 30% and our budget by 40%. The organization still feels the repercussions of those decisions and is still climbing back to the position it held before the economy crashed. However, if we hadn't made those tough decisions, the organization wouldn't be around at all.

As you move forward with your venture, realize that you can do all the planning in the world and still face hard times beyond your control. Although you can take many steps to protect yourself, you can't save your venture from certain tragedies. Instead of despairing, do everything you can to expect the unexpected and prepare for the unknown.

What could prevent your venture from succeeding?

49 | Minimize Your Controllable Obstacles

A number of underlying threats to your venture exist WITHIN your control. For example, if you are not the best at managing money and you've always had a track record for struggling with this issue, this could hinder your long-term success. As revenues begin to flow and your business expands, the growth could actually challenge you. Growth without money management equals failure. If you struggle with money, you'll need to surround yourself with people who manage money well, understand checks and balances, know how to read a balance sheet and income statement, operate with integrity, and have your best interest in mind. Without this, you're doomed.

How and who you hire can be another avoidable barrier. In my work with a number of professional athletes, I've seen countless ideas go up in flames due to fragmentation in relationships, hiring processes and poor decision-making. Athletes often hire unqualified family members, friends and acquaintances. The number one excuse I hear for these decisions is that they want to hire people they trust. Ironically, they discover the hard way that these people aren't trustworthy at all when it comes to fundamental business practices. It's one thing to trust someone as a friend or family member, but it's entirely different to trust them in a business context. Athletes' poor hiring decisions waste millions of dollars and hundreds of great ideas. Whatever you do, work diligently to not fall into the same trap.

Make wise hiring decisions. Have trustworthy people around you who understand what it takes to launch a new organization or business. Consult your local Society of Human Resource Management (SHRM) to see if they have someone willing to help you establish good hiring practices, job descriptions, policies, and procedures.

After you've hired trusted employees, you'll need to lead and keep them. It's easy to lose great talent. You have to invest in your employees, respect them, provide them with a healthy work culture, avoid micromanaging them, and surround them with integrity. If you don't intentionally create a culture that appeals to great talent, you'll have difficulty keeping great talent. Read books, attend seminars, find coaches and mentors, survey your team, and do everything imaginable to attract and support talent.

You can control other threats to your venture including poor customer service, low quality products, a poor service delivery model, hasty growth, insufficient infra-structure and a lack of focus. Look for examples of failure and success in business. Identify two or three people from each of the two outcomes and ask if they'd keep an ongoing dialogue with you as you move forward with your venture. Here are some questions you'll want to ask them:

- How did you structure your businesses?

- What would you do differently?

- Who did you hire and why?

- How did you manage cash flow?

- How did you sustain quality control?

- How did you correct errors in judgment?

You can learn a lot from those who have traveled the path ahead of you. Learn from these people *before* you rush into your venture. There are enough chal-lenges outside your control, so take advantage of the ones within your control.

What obstacles exist WITHIN your control?

50 | Face Your Uncontrollable Obstacles

There are many factors BEYOND your control that could cause devastation to your success. A friend of mine from Memphis, Tennessee, ran a printing company a couple of decades ago, but success actually became the uncontrollable force that killed his business. In his best days of operating, 80% of his revenues came from small businesses where employees could manage accounts and make themselves accessible. They could communicate and resolve problems rapidly because all parties had the freedom and flexibility of a small business. He continued to win clients, and his dreams came true – or so he thought. He landed FedEx as a client and began pulling back on some of the smaller clients to focus on the new big customer. Soon he found the large print jobs FedEx placed with him drained his revenue. The jobs tied up his capital, and FedEx gave a turnaround on Accounts Payable of 90 to 120 days, *when* they would pay him. He couldn't control his client's response time, and this one client was eating up his operating capital. This put him in a vulnerable position as an operator. This uncontrollable situation destroyed his business. Who would've thought that too much success too soon could actually hurt you?

You will encounter situations beyond your control, which might hinder your development cycles. Don't think you're invincible or that catastrophe can only happen to *other* people. Many people make this mistake, and their lack of paranoia leads to their destruction.

If you start a trucking company, you cannot regulate oil and gas prices. If you launch a car wash in Seattle, you cannot control the rain. If you form a lemonade stand in Alaska, you cannot control the outdoor climate. You can be the most talented person in a specific market, but you simply cannot control everything. Brace yourself for the out-of-control factors.

What obstacles exist BEYOND your control?

51 | Overcome Your Contradictions

So, you will have barriers to success no matter the level of greatness for you or your venture. Some of the barriers will be within your control, and others will be outside of your control. Either way, you need to plan your method for attacking these issues.

Take some time right now to list eight to ten things you see as the greatest obstacles you will face on a separate sheet of paper. Then, narrow your list down to what you would consider to be your greatest three issues. After narrowing down your list to your top three, please list them in the "problem" areas at the end of this section. Here are some challenges you might consider:

- human capital
- finances
- product development
- board of directors
- time commitment
- fear of failure
- space limitations
- facilities
- logistics

When you finish writing out your problem, outline three steps you can take to begin overcoming each barrier. For example, suppose one of your greatest barriers is finance related. Here is how you would list the barrier and possible solutions.

Problem:
> Limited Financial Resources

Steps to Address the Problem:

1) Visit The Small Business Association and a lending institution to discuss options for raising additional capital.

2) Attend a local seminar that addresses raising capital during the start-up phase of a business.

3) Do extensive research and develop a financial feasibility plan.

You could continue this list, but you don't want to become overwhelmed and end up talking yourself out of your plans. Start with two or three main barriers. Once you've addressed those issues, you can add others to the list. If you need more space, grab some scratch paper and begin working through additional problems and solution steps.

Problem 1:

_____

Steps to Address the Problem:

1)_____

2)_____

3)_____

Problem 2:

_____

Steps to Address the Problem:

1)_____

2)_____

3)_____

Problem 3:

_____

Steps to Address the Problem:

1)_____

2)_____

3)_____

What 3 to 5 underlying contradictions do you have to overcome?

"**Brace yourself** for the **Out-of-Control Factors**

Step Eight:
Differentiating Your Brand

Step Eight:
Differentiating Your Brand

One of my favorite books of all time is *ZAG* by Marty Neumeier. He explains the strange title of his book in the excerpt below:

> *As the pace of business quickens and the number of brands multiplies, it's customers, not companies, who decide which brands live and which brands die. An overabundance of look-alike products and me-too services is forcing customers to search for something, anything, to help them separate winners from the clutter. The solution? When everybody zigs, ZAG!*

I love Marty's perspective on "zagging" vs. "zigging." I'm not sure Ralph Lauren products are any better than Old Navy products in terms of quality. Yet, the average consumer pays more for a Ralph Lauren shirt than an Old Navy shirt. Ralph Lauren has mastered the ability to differentiate their brand. The irony in their strategy is that in addition to the consumers they intentionally target, their differentiated brand also hooks a lower financial tier of consumers who've also bought into the brand. Ralph Lauren's target demographics include professionals with an affluent life of sailing, horseback riding, and playing rugby or polo. But they also target the much larger market of people who want to associate with prestige and luxury. We call this larger market their target psychographics.

As you think about your launch or expansion, narrow the demographics and psychographics of your target customer. You have to narrow them down because if you try to be all things to all people you'll end up being nothing to no one. There are ways around this issue, but you have to carve out a niche for your concept, organization, or business.

Keep in mind that the smaller the niche, the more important it is for you to differentiate your brand. For example, if you want to become the dominant brand in the soft drink, denim, or salad dressing markets, you have a lot of big names to compete with. These markets are highly competitive, difficult to penetrate and costly to acquire initial customers. Such a dream is not impossible but it is implausible. You could spend your life, and two to three generations more, trying to accomplish this mission. An established, multi-billion dollar company in a beverage market could eat you alive. This doesn't mean you can't create the next big thing. Twitter didn't exist a decade ago, but today it holds a market cap valuation of just under $30 billion and trades at just under $50 a share. The tech market is unique in its fast turn-over. Another decade from now, Twitter could cease to exist. With that success they are currently having, it does not appear likely but we have seen it happen previously. A number of Fortune 500 Companies have gone extinct less than a decade after a high value rating. American President Lines and Standard Register, companies I interned with in college, once led their industries but disappeared five years later. The market is agile and consumers are fickle. You have to be willing to pivot when the market says pivot, and you must intentionally pursue differentiation.

A differentiation strategy is one of the best advantages you can give your venture. Make a list of several concepts, organizations or companies you consider leaders in their industries. Determine what catapulted them to the top. Study their successes and failures, their ability to pivot, and the qualities that appeal to their customers. Do a comprehensive comparative analysis. As you learn from them, look for ways to apply the same principles to your enterprise.

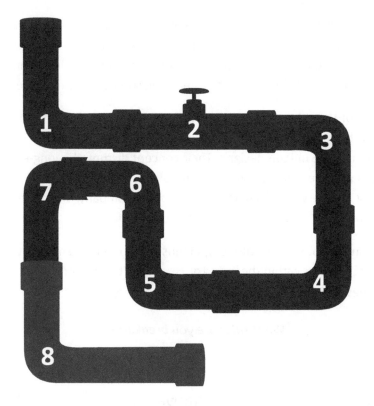

52 | Break the Rules

Great concepts emerge when a leader develops a novel solution to a problem. Some of the best and brightest ideas have been rule breaking in scope. Great leaders like Bill Gates, Steve Jobs, Peter Thiel and Mark Zuckerberg completely disrupted cycles of commerce and entrepreneurship by deviating from tradition.

Rules create boxes around all kinds of markets including education, politics, ministry, government, non-profit, medicine and many others that need innovation. Regardless of where your concept fits, be disruptive and unorthodox in your approach. Create something new or solve a problem in a new way. Step outside the norm.

One simple way to begin innovating is to poll your target market and ask them what they desire. Threadless T's built their entire business model on their customers' ideas. In the saturated t-shirt market, Threadless decided to put a unique spin on production. They placed the power in the hands of the consumer by holding ongoing competitions for the consumer to submit their design ideas. Once consumers submit their ideas, their peers vote and the winning designers receive cash prizes from Threadless. Even better than the cash, Threadless produces the winning t-shirt, so the designer can walk down the street and see someone wearing their design.

The founders of Threadless came up with a simple, yet powerful method to rapidly expand their business. They produce high-quality t-shirts, meet their customers' needs, and promote unique designs. Their concept disrupted a long-established industry and gathered market share in one of the most competitive spaces for market entry. If I interviewed a team member of the company, one piece of advice they would probably give is to "break conventional rules."

Think of business models that will disrupt industries. In fact, you might even create an entirely new sector within the industry. Heck, don't stop there, why not create an entirely new industry? Be daring, be bold, be different. Break all the rules!

What rules are you breaking?

53 | Highlight Your Concept's Innovation

Maybe you've decided to compete with Ford, Coke, Facebook, Mrs. Fields Cookies, McDonald's or some other industry leader. Or maybe you intend to simply localize your business and avoid competing at that level. This second option is wise at the onset of your venture because you might find there's no demand in your area. Regardless of your competitors' size, you'll need to clarify what makes your concept special.

Many consider Memphis, Tennessee, to be the home of the BBQ Restaurant market. In a city with a metro population of approximately 1.3 million people, BBQ consumers have hundreds of options. With all the market saturation of BBQ restaurants, let's imagine you decide to start another one and your goal is for your restaurant to be the best in the city. Maybe you expect success because of a secret sauce, your leadership dynamics, your location or your method for smoking the food. You'll still have to ask, "Why on earth would customers who are already loyal to their favorite BBQ joint(s) want to convert to my restaurant?"

You probably won't have an answer overnight. Customer acquisition challenges most business and non-profit owners. People have options, so you have to continually pursue brand distinction, especially in the early stages of your concept. Not only are you competing with those who have a pre-existing platform in the market, you're also competing against "Joe Schmoe" who's entering the market the same time as you and also thinks he has the best idea. Always think with competitive creativity at the forefront of your imagination.

What makes you so special?

54 | Form Your Effective Brand

Think about the number of decisions you've made in your life, both good and bad, that have been emotionally driven. Sadness, anger, joy, exuberance, humor, offense, greed, hunger, desire, passion, and other emotions influence each of us to make decisions that can sometimes lead to less than desirable outcomes. I cannot tell you the number of people I have sat down with who have made decisions based on their emotions only to come back later and feel an alternate emotion of regret, disappointment, or hurt.

Fractl is a full-service digital marketing agency that specializes in content marketing and social media. *The Harvard Business Review, Forbes, Fast Company*, and many other reputable sources have featured them. In their research on "The Emotions that Make Marketing Campaigns Go Viral," they found emotions play an important role in marketing and branding strategy. In fact, they listed the top ten and bottom ten emotions that companies can leverage for success:

Top 10 Positive Emotions:

- Amusement
- Interest
- Surprise
- Happiness
- Delight
- Pleasure
- Joy

- Hope
- Affection
- Excitement

Bottom 10 Emotions:
- Anger
- Politeness
- Frustration
- Doubt
- Embarrassment
- Despair
- Hurt
- Guilt
- Contempt
- Shame

What emotion do you want to convey? If you convey guilt, contempt, or shame, your odds of success are low. However, amusement, interest, or surprise will likely generate customer interest. Think long and hard about the type of emotion you want to convey as you think about your brand identity.

What emotion do you want your brand to convey?

55 | Form Your Unique Brand

Don't confuse your product or service's distinguishing value proposition with your brand's distinguishing value proposition. For TOMS shoes, the product offering is *shoes* but the distinguishing brand proposition is *charity*. Blake Mycoskie's "buy a shoe/give a shoe" model has drastically influenced the world of social enterprise initiatives. Now, TOMS dominates the charity shoe market. Since the burgeoning of TOMS, numerous other brands have begun similar work in various industries. TOMS exploded from its original, simple canvas shoe to a brand that now includes sunglasses, coffee, boots and fashion accessories. Everything follows the buy-one-give-one model that has revolutionized the way people do business and interact with brands.

The Millennials and Gen Y'ers support profits with a purpose, companies that express a deliberate cause for what they do. Companies that evolve with the modern, transitional world will thrive with these new generations. As you think about the unique value proposition your brand can bring to your target market, consider who your market is, what they value, and whether you can draw zealots from them. To create zealots, you have to engage your audience and attempt to infiltrate their lifestyle. As you attempt to solve a problem for them, associate your brand with this problem-solving action. In today's climate, if you operate for money alone, you'll lose an entire generation of young people who will one day possess wealth and decision-making power. Many of today's youth, in fact, already influence entire markets. Social media and the Internet allow young people to spread product reviews faster and wider than ever. Now, the average, everyday consumer possesses the power to determine whether a brand succeeds or fails. Consider the type of brand value you want to evoke and begin deliberating how to shape a corporate culture that evokes that value.

What is your brand's unique contribution to the marketplace?

56 | Create a Memorable Image for Your Business

One of the best ways you can inspire brand optimism is to communicate powerfully through your logo design. When it comes to your logo, beauty is in the eye of the beholder. Your logo will either compel or repel the beholder, so you have to make sure they leave with an impression that matches the message you intended to convey. You want your logo to tell an effective story.

Most people will encounter a visual depiction of what you represent instead of you personally. We do this every time we judge a person without knowing them. The average person bases their initial impression of others purely on the person's appearance. This explains why you see a gorgeous lady and think, *She's gorgeous* or a handsome guy and think, *He's handsome*. When making these internal decisions about people, you base your decision solely on external factors and features. You size them up; stare them down; glance at their shoes, pants, shirt, hair color, eyes, facial structure, tone of voice, body language; and you make your judgment. We determine a person's attractiveness within moments of that first glance.

The same is true for products and services. People will judge you based on a quick glance. In his blog (www.kissmetrics.com) entitled "How Do Colors Affect Purchases?" Kissmetrics explained that 93% of consumers believe visual appearance and color influence buyers more than any other factor. Additionally, 85% of consumers stated color had everything to do with their buying a particular product, and 80% believed color increases brand recognition. As you develop your logo or have someone else develop your logo, think about what you want to convey at first glance. For example, the United Way's logo exemplifies an open hand helping a small person (person in need) along with helping people of all colors. The logo tells their mission without any explanation.

Begin thinking what you want your logo to convey. Here are some factors to think about:

- Size
- Shapes
- Colors
- Emotions
- Font(s)
- Wording
- Imagery

See if you can find out why successful businesses chose their logos. Reach out to branding departments of major corporations. Talk to artists, brand designers, photographers, and other creative geniuses about what goes into their creation process. While you don't need to spend an inordinate amount of time on your logo, you do want to take this step seriously. Your logo has the power to singlehandedly influence buyers. There is power in a logo.

What are your ideas around your logo and brand imagery?

57 | Promote Your Business

Once you've worked through your visual components, you can begin drafting your plan for advertising and promoting your business.

One of the worst mistakes you can make is to attempt to promote your brand without having any written plan. Recall who you want to reach with your product or service and how you plan to engage that demographic. Once again, although you'll long for everyone to see your brand as their go-to brand, not everyone will. You simply can't appeal to every person on the planet, nor are you ready to serve every person on the planet. In your startup, you're barely in a position to service the first 1% of those who will ultimately become loyal to your brand. Carve out a segment of the market and your specific target demographic within that market. From there, develop a reasonable plan to reach that corner of the market.

After you've refocused your audience, prepare to invest a lot of time, talent, and money to introduce your brand to the masses. Like most people, you might struggle to secure capital. Luckily, we have a new asset: the Internet! People all over the world have built businesses by utilizing sources like Facebook, Twitter, Instagram, or just pure search engine optimization. Use these inexpensive resources in your promotion plan. You don't need a multi-million-dollar budget to get out of the gate. You need a multi-million-dollar idea that will attract investors.

Although you have the Internet for publicity, don't skimp on your advertisement investments. You'll want to dedicate 10%-15% of your capital to advertising and promotions. Develop this spending discipline early on because you'll always need to out-innovate and out-think your competitors. When you can't compete financially with large prominent entities, you can compete in creativity. Still, even creative ideas will take some capital.

Whether you plan to develop a product, launch a non-profit, or start a small business, you'll need to target trade shows, pitch events, conferences, and other environments that provide exposure. Time is your greatest commodity, so use it wisely.

While promoting your brand, think about people you have in your inner circle who can champion your brand. If you have people with expertise in marketing, branding, or promoting, call on them for support. Depending on the type of product, organization, or business, large or boutique advertising firms and marketing agencies sometimes offer their expertise as *pro bono* work. Some boutique, start-up firms might do an initial project for you with the understanding that when you begin generating capital, you'll compensate them. You can also find college students willing to volunteer in order to gain experience and strengthen their resume. Look for those advertisers whose mission fits with your work. If they turn you down, don't take it personally.

Upon founding The Gifted Education Foundation, I had very limited financial resources. However, a friend and his team supported us in developing our first round of promotional materials. We agreed that as our foundation grew, we would compensate those who initially volunteered their services. This demonstrates the importance of making friends. Honor your connections, operate with integrity and never burn bridges. You never know if you'll need them in the future.

The supporters of The Gifted Education Foundation invested in our work because they trusted I would deliver on my commitment. Prepare for the commitment before you engage anyone's services, regardless of how small the contribution may seem to you. Treat all contributions as grand as the largest contribution. This builds a group of champions for your brand.

The last bit of advice I have for you on this subject is to believe in your brand. Exhibit passion and charge the hill in order to spread the word about your offering. If you don't believe in it, you won't convince others to believe in it. And if you can't convince others to believe in it, you don't stand a chance at capturing market share. It all starts with your leadership and confidence. Develop your plan, believe in it and execute it.

How will you promote your business?

Step Nine:
Developing Human Capital

Step Nine:
Developing Human Capital

Your ability to select, train, and retain good employees won't automatically bring you success, but these skills do factor into the equation. You'll only go as far as the people who surround you. People are your greatest asset.

You need people to help you execute the critical components of your venture. These people cannot be just any people; they need to be the RIGHT people. They'll provoke you, but they'll also inspire you. They'll create problems, but they'll also solve problems. You'll take the roller coaster ride of your life attempting to lead them. John Maxwell, one of the greatest gurus of leadership, said, "Everything rises and falls on leadership." If you plan to proceed with your idea and sustain it long-term, you'll need a developed and well-led team. You can only get so far on your brilliant ideas, good looks, charming character and even financial capital. Human capital is everything.

The first step to leading a great team is to be a great leader. I've spoken to thousands of people on various platforms and the one piece of advice I frequently give is that you cannot lead where you are not willing to go, and you cannot teach what you don't know. It all starts with you. From there, you can invest in the people around you, developing them just like you develop your venture.

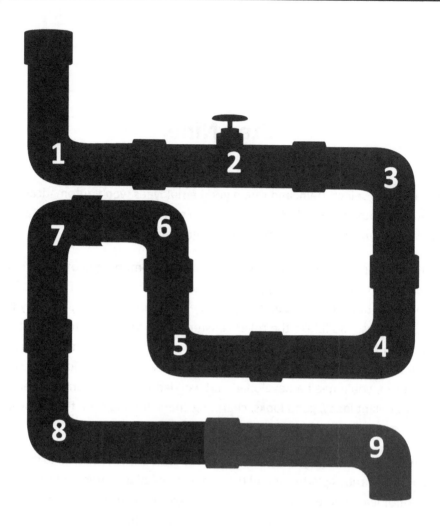

58 | Assess Your Qualifications

For the last several years, I have tuned in to *American Idol* to see underdogs from small towns in Nowhere, USA, burst onto the scene with explosive talent. Among this talent each season, thousands of others emerge but take for granted the skill required to ultimately be "America's Idol." It blows my mind that every year so many of these people show up without having someone in their inner circle who has the courage to advise them not to waste their time, money and breath aiming for what appears to be an unrealistic goal. I support risks and having faith in your dream but not when it guarantees failure. At that point, faith becomes foolishness.

I'm sure you can think of people in your past who were preparing to step in a direction you knew would doom them to failure. In fact, you might know someone in that position now. That person might even be you! Give the people around you permission to speak truth in your life. You're better off knowing now if the path ahead of you is paved with landmines. Don't pursue a doomed path out of pride or ignorance. Take educated risks but avoid foolish ones.

To measure risks, examine your qualifications honestly. People with great ideas, a tremendous plan, a supportive team and all the necessary capital still struggle with unexpected obstacles. Thousands of ideas rise and fall annually, and some of the sharpest people lead them. Of course, failure comes with entrepreneurship. Your business heroes would probably tell you they found success *in spite of* failures not because they never failed. Since even well-prepared leaders struggle, you know the challenge is great. Capital will dwindle, employees will turn their backs on you, deals will slip through the cracks, and projections will go unfulfilled. Assess how well you satisfy the expected qualifications, passion and willpower to press through storms when they rise. These assessments help determine the risk level.

Just as important as internal will is your external skill. You can have all the passion and determination in the world, but if you struggle with math and science, the odds of you becoming a rocket scientist don't weigh in your favor. If you've only dropped fries at a local fast food restaurant, you can't expect to start a world-renowned business in a year. Your dream needs to align with your resume and work history. In addition to specific skills, you'll need to exhibit exceptional work ethic. Do a 360-degree self-assessment to determine whether you can manage the task at hand.

Even if you do possess the qualifications for the job, don't go forward in isolation. Surround yourself with family, friends, board members, co-workers and educators who are fully vested in you. Invite them onto the journey. Even if you don't fully embrace their input, they can provide an objective viewpoint to challenge you. If nothing else, these unique perspectives will keep you grounded, humble and hungry to learn.

Are you qualified to deliver on this assignment

59 | Evaluate Your Personal Threats

One of the greatest barriers to long-term success is when entrepreneurs unknowingly hinder their own success.

Arrogance, pride, unrealistic expectations and a lack of accountability can all work against your own venture. Sadly, we often know about these flaws but refuse to change them. Professional athletes never stop training and never stop receiving coaching. Even the Most Valuable Players recognize the power of continuous learning. Whether you are an unusually talented athlete, educator, Navy Seal, motivational speaker, truck driver or horticulturist, in most cases, your greatness will not be tied to talent alone. Talent contributes to success, but unusual work ethic, discipline and other intrinsic qualities carry far more weight than natural talent.

Ray Lewis, a retired National Football League player with the Baltimore Ravens, is arguably the greatest defensive player to ever play the sport at a professional level. Based on the number of personal interactions I've had with him, I can tell you that two things separated Ray from the other professional football players: 1) his willingness to allow the pain of his past to drive his leadership and 2) his work ethic. While he clearly had natural talent, the talent alone was never enough. The NFL always has a long list of talented athletes. What the NFL does not always have is a list of talented athletes who will last more than a decade and a half playing such a brutal sport, especially at the linebacker position. Ray faced every obstacle you can imagine, as an athlete and as a person. Despite his struggles, he classified the obstacles as opportunities. He didn't let people deny him, and he didn't let his circumstances define him. Instead of running from the storms in his life, Ray turned toward the storms and used them as inspirational leverage. He made mistakes, but he turned his story into one of trial to triumph. He resisted becoming his own worst enemy and used the pain of his story to fuel his success.

How will you leverage your pain and obstacles to inspire you? Even better than talent and work ethic is the capacity to use challenges to change, stretch and grow against all odds. Embrace constructive feedback. Not everyone has the courage to walk with this humility, but visible flaws we ignore are less dangerous than invisible flaws we don't recognize. We call these flaws blind spots, and if left unattended, they can create serious barriers to success.

If you don't have people to draw your attention to your blind spots, you will continually walk a fine line between success and failure. The stories of failure outnumber the success stories. Think of the students voted "most likely to succeed" in high school who fall short of those expectations today. Personality and ideas can only take you so far before you'll need to display tangible elements of execution. Quality leadership ultimately ties to your willingness to innovate, stretch, grow, and adapt relative to your personal areas of growth.

In his book *What Got You Here, Won't Get You There*, Marshall Goldsmith explains why high achievers have such trouble with long-term success. According to Goldsmith, they rely so heavily on previous successes that they fail to realize that the path to previous success is not *always* the path to future success. As a leader, you have to deliberately fight the temptation to believe your own press clippings. Don't allow small victories, or even large ones, to build you up so much that you lose the humble fire that got you started. Complacency stalks you right along with the competitor that threatens to smother you.

Continually watch for signs that you've become your own enemy. It happens far more often than you realize. Don't be the next one to cause your own destruction.

Could you be your own worst enemy?

60 | Position Yourself According to Your Natural Skills

Recall once again Bob Shank's three types of people: originators, organizers and operators. Usually these go in sequential order. The originators, the idea people, see a problem and create a solution. Then the organizers add shape and definition to the originators' basic idea. Finally, the operators give the project its consistency and sustainability.

Enlist the help of some close friends and conduct a self-assessment. Calculate what percent of each personality type you are. You might be 50% originator and 50% organizer or 10% originator, 60% organizer, and 30% operator. Resist the temptation to believe you're 100% of all three. You cannot work proficiently in all three areas. Determine the one or two categories that you operate in most effectively. Then, find an equally committed person who's skilled in the areas you lack.

If you're a dominant originator (60% or more), position yourself where you can spend the majority of your time innovating. If you're a dominant organizer, leave the inventing to the originator and focus on building on the originator's ideas. If you're a dominant operator, set up the right systems, metrics, people and other logistics needed for sustainability. Respect the other groups but focus on the task most aligned with your personality. If you happen to possess a healthy balance of a couple of these attributes, get in where you fit in but set up boundaries that remind you to let others lead in their areas of strength. Know your role and lean into your strengths.

Are you an originator, organizer or operator?

61 | Measure Your Human Capital

While my education supported my path toward entrepreneurship, my life experiences have equipped me most of all.

The Gifted Education Foundation has a mission to produce marketplace leaders from low-income communities across America. While many business savvy people could run this organization, I have some personal experiences that elevate my qualifications to lead such a movement. I've experienced poverty first hand. Born to a teenage mother and coming from an incredibly fragmented family, I've spent my life living in or surrounded by poverty. Many of my current connections directly tie to my upbringing along with some close family that still lives in these conditions. My past, along with my education, business acumen, and non-profit leadership gives me an edge on others who might enter the same space. I've chosen to use my background as leverage and continue leaning into it as opposed to running from it. I continue to discover more about myself through reading, taking personality profiles, working with mentors, absorbing executive coaching, and working through rigorous life and personal planning.

A number of resources are available to support you on your journey of personal discovery. For example, the Gallup Organization has produced a number of books. I recommend starting with their *StrengthsFinder* series. I took the *StrengthsFinder* assessment and learned about my natural behaviors and preferences. To give just one example, people teased me about my love for learning as a child. When I took the *StrengthsFinder* assessment, I discovered my top strength is "Input," making me an information sponge. In addition to Input, I scored high in Analytical, Strategic, Activator, and Woo (Winning Others Over). This knowledge about myself better prepares me to find specific ways I can add value to my community.

Take time to discover what makes you tick. Begin by mapping out your childhood, family lineage, education, training, certifications, books you've read, and anything else that could give you an edge on your path to success. The general knowledge you get from educational, corporate, and other conventional systems won't nec- essarily reveal *the real* you. These systems prepare you to learn how to function within their confines and don't necessarily empower you to become self-sufficient. You have to make it a priority to learn about yourself and the value you bring.

What unique human capital assets do you offer?

62 | Measure Your Team's Human Capital

Mature leaders assess not only themselves but also their leadership team. Many leaders focus so much on what's in it for them that they fail to cultivate the talents of those they work with. You have to determine whether you want to see subtrac- tion, addition, or multiplication as it pertains to the growth and expansion of your venture. Some products or concepts offer enough on their own to keep average workers. These workers will stay on board as long as they get a steady paycheck and see some progress. The progress you'll see will probably be simple addition, a steady but slow growth. On the other hand, if you want to make the shift from leading followers to leading leaders, you'll need to invest in your personal growth as well as the growth of your team members. When development becomes your priority, you'll experience multiplication, a much faster growth.

Talent won't be enough on its own. You have to invest in those with the talent. Your concept might have the potential to revolutionize the industry, but it will never take off without the right people to execute it. Do whatever it takes to recruit, train and retain great talent.

What unique human capital assets does your team offer?

63 | Establish Proper Leadership

Even best-in-class business leaders sometimes lack the specific skills for running a non-profit. I'm a living example that it can be done, but not everyone is cut out for non-profit work. This work requires far more energy than you imagine and requires you to work with fewer resources. Some of the best salesmen and greatest business leaders lack the ability to motivate unpaid people. You wield more leverage when directing people who show up because they have to than you do for people who show up because they have a fleeting desire to follow you.

I took a huge step by exiting corporate America years ago and focusing on non-profit work. My upbringing didn't prepare me for the journey, and while my academic preparation, business degree, and professional work provided me some universal skills, those skills didn't specifically translate to this new line of work. I shifted from a focus on revenues generated to a focus on community outreach and had to adjust my skills as a result.

In my very first non-profit assignment, I realized I had shifted into a role where I was younger and far less experienced than the volunteers and eventual staff members on my leadership team. Because of my inexperience, I practically lost an entire team of volunteers. I knew I had to either step up or step out. I wasn't about to step out. Though I faced one of the greatest seasons of stress in my life, I wouldn't accept failure. I read twenty-six books in 2002, attended seminars, fought to secure mentors, and did everything imaginable to save my venture. I knew I couldn't lead where I wasn't willing to go, and I couldn't teach anyone else what I didn't know. For me to *put out*, I had to *put in*. I had to put in hours of personal development as I studied ministry, non-profits, development procedures, fundraising strategies and ways to impact a transitioning community. I mapped community assets, went to local high schools, talked to business and community leaders, met with church leaders, and most importantly, I met with students who fit the demographic I wanted to serve. It was a messy process for a 24-year-old young man who was a wreck internally. I was trying to figure out my own life while helping others figure out theirs. We were all *growing up* together.

Your venture will require a lot of sweat and thousands of hours learning, growing, struggling and triumphing. As the leader of your venture, you have to commit to the long journey regardless of the challenges. If the mission doesn't compel you to this mentality, you need to exit before you bite off more than you can chew. If you want your business and the world around you to improve, start by improving yourself.

If you're not the right person for the assignment, who is?

64 | Build Your Team

Your venture might be a one-man show or you could have a fully operative machine with several staff members hanging on for dear life. Regardless of which position you find yourself in, you should always be developing the team around you.

If you start your venture alone, at some point either you'll wear out or your venture will suffer. You only have 100% of you to give, and even that has limitations. There are only 168 hours in a week, and unless you never sleep, never eat, never interact with people, and never have a personal life, you'll only give a portion of this time to your venture. You're going to need the time, talent, resources, networks, and ideas of a team.

Not everyone will carry the passion you have for your concept. Therefore, you'll need to develop a long-term strategy that allows you to optimize the people around you while giving them a sense of fulfillment. If this ain't happening, they ain't staying.

In addition to a killer idea, you need strategy and willingness to establish and grow a team. Once again, these are not necessarily skills you gain from everyday life or college. Most work cultures don't even emphasize people development as much as they emphasize product or idea development. So if you feel like a fish out of water in this area, it's probably because you are a fish out of water in this area. That's okay, as long as you do something about it. Make the necessary adjustments so you can put a healthy team and infrastructure in place. You cannot hire people and then abandon them. You have to invest in their professional and personal growth. Invest in yourself and invest in your people. This is the only path to long-term success.

What steps are you taking to build your team?

65 | Develop Your Leadership

Every year in December, I pull away for a few days and prepare a comprehensive plan for the next year. This planning process involves strategizing goals for my community involvement and my personal, family, career, and spiritual life. I also lay out organizational plans, which includes setting goals and a strategy for my leadership team.

Many of the best organizations gain their reputation because of their leadership pipeline and human capital development strategy. You have to take intentional steps to develop the leaders in your inner circle. This will help you maintain healthy team chemistry, productivity and innovation. Many organizations and businesses with underdeveloped leadership will limp for a season, but eventually the tide rolls and poor infrastructure comes crashing down. As you develop yourself and your team, you must develop your leaders.

All this developing time might feel overwhelming, but you cannot afford to ignore leadership development. If for no other reason, challenging the leaders in your inner circle helps you weed out the weak links. I've had people kick and scream about having to stretch themselves. As it turned out, I never had to eliminate these people from the teams I led. They eliminated themselves. Whether it was moral failure, burnout, failure to hit objectives, or some other reason, the laggards knew when to remove themselves. While success is not guaranteed, it's also not accidental. As long as you continue personal growth and development as well as organizational growth and development, you'll continually improve your odds of success. You have to intentionally develop a winning team with winning leaders.

Begin mapping out your plan. In addition to bi-weekly conference calls where we share leadership and personal development strategies, every sixty days our team gathers to do a "State of the Union" meeting. People share books, news articles, Scriptures, blogs, and/or internally developed ideas in advance so the team has time to meditate on the content. Then, for four hours, everyone is required to participate. Most people walk away energized, recharged, and ready to take on the world. Again, those who are not willing to engage the process will usually weed themselves out. This process works best for our team because we have an organized human capital infrastructure. I encourage you to survey your volunteers, current leaders, and even people thinking of joining forces with you. The information you gather will help you determine the best process for developing your team. In the end, your process might differ from ours. Just seek the best development strategy for your leadership team. There is no magic formula except to have a formula.

What is your leadership development strategy?

66 | Acquire Talent

You likely have people around you who strive to accomplish the work you want to accomplish. We say these people have the same spirit of *achieving* what you want to achieve. These people might not have the passion you have, though. Those who match your passion for your work have the same spirit of *desiring* what you desire.

The size of your talent pool will depend on the type of idea or work you pursue. Either way, you'll need to develop a talent acquisition pipeline. When I pursue talent, I group people in three categories depending on the value they bring to the project.

The first category, the "bottom third," are those people who want to help but lack the ability. You probably won't use all these people, so you have to learn to recognize those who don't suit your project. This takes incredible discipline to say no to people who "feel" they can help. People who fall into this category can appear to have great personality, skills, chemistry, etc. However, you cannot make the assumption that because someone has seen success in one field they can bring success to your endeavors. For example, a successful operator in an institutional enterprise that has been around for years might struggle in your enterprise when it's still in the idea stages. The people, resources, and talent will look completely different in your context than in that individual's previous context. Again, you'll need restraint because sometimes, the people that belong in your bottom third happen to be the "lowest hanging fruit." They're accessible and might even crave the opportunity to participate in your work. They might help someday, but if you hire a "bottom third" person too soon, your long-term development could fall apart.

The middle third category consists of the people who could transition either to the top third or the bottom third. These people blend natural talent, shared values, and shared chemistry for the cause. As you continue to expand your reach, these individuals will either expand with you or fall back when they can no longer keep up with the changes. You can determine which way to move these people by continually delegating greater responsibilities to them as your organization, business or product scales. This sounds simple but it's not an easy task. We tend to function according to status quo even in the midst of acceleration or deceleration. Because we don't stop to assess where we are and plan for where we're heading, leaders can fail to place people in the proper categories. In such cases, we'll either waste the talent or lose it to a better leader. On the flipside, people who don't have the bandwidth or desire to go to the next level can end up hanging around longer than they should. This can lower the bar for everyone, ultimately leading to poor performance. If you want to grow your concept, organization, or business, you have to intentionally develop the "middle third."

Finally, the buck stops with your "top third" tier of talent. It doesn't usually take a lot of time for individuals that fall into this category to determine whether your work fits them. In many ways, they're unorthodox, wildly creative, hungry, entrepreneurial, results oriented, and even have the capacity to do your job better than you in many areas. Seek these people out. You need them for success.

You'll face challenges while finding and hiring top-third people. First and foremost, you have to be a secure enough leader to guide members of this category. Otherwise you'll fail and they'll likely go do a better job than you at what you attempted.

Keep in mind that people who fall into this top category will challenge you, your ideas, your processes and your systems. And that's why you need them. You won't always have the answers. You need other people who are smarter, stronger, and wiser than you. If you're always the smartest person in the room, get out of that room swiftly or change the room around. Keep your eyes open for exceptional people who are doing exceptional things that can add value to your venture. Again, you have to pursue personal growth and development or two things will happen: you won't recognize this top level of talent, and if you do recognize it, you'll be intimidated by those who possess it.

Keep an open mind as you meet people and continue to sharpen your capacity to determine whether they're a bottom, middle or top tier leader. You cannot accomplish what you ultimately want to accomplish without exceptional leaders in your corner and to recognize them you have to know how to categorize your supporters.

What is your talent acquisition strategy?

67 | Retain Talent

In addition to growth and development strategies, you'll need a talent retention strategy.

One of my favorite books is *What Got You Here, Won't Get You There* by Marshall Goldsmith. The book explains how many leaders assume the same path of success they took to get to their current destination will keep them moving to the next level. History has shown time and time again this is not the case. In fact, you can probably recall moments of your own life where you had to make some radical adjustments to get to the next level. Change is an unavoidable and necessary constant. As the leader of your venture, if you don't evolve with the global economy, your venture will die. Additionally, if you're not deliberate about evolving and retaining the exceptional talent you recruit, your organization or business will fail.

Another way you can lose talent is by allowing the wrong environment to burn talented people out. They need surroundings that sync with their personal growth. As the leader, you'll have to provide for this need. Consider the frequency and structure of your staff meetings, quarterly planning sessions, staff leadership retreats, book and article readings, conferences, and other supportive tools. These assets form the supportive surroundings that inspire great leaders to thrive.

One last warning: don't lose combinations of talent and good work ethic when you find them. This combination is rare in our modern culture where everyone wants everything right now. We live in a microwave and quick fix society that replaces the values of the past with schemes and scandals. When you find people with talent and scruples, you better find a way to hold on to them. Others will try to steal that talent from you.

Recall the rule of leadership I gave you earlier: good leaders lead followers, but great leaders lead leaders. To attract great leaders, you need to prepare a strategy. You can't just wing it and expect the most talented and capable leaders to show up at your doorstep. Sketch the kind of supportive environment you want for your leaders and formulate a plan for achieving it.

What's your talent retention strategy?

68 | Staff Your Team Sufficiently

Leaders have to evaluate and assess growth strategies and staffing needs for their businesses. Only then can they properly assess current issues and determine the best solution to future problems.

I've worked with a number of professional athletes and have seen many of them experience catastrophes when hiring staff for their businesses and organizations. One of the problems I see is that instead of learning the business or non-profit field, many athletes use their income to hire others to do the work for them. I've witnessed the waste of such spending. They hire people because of familiarity instead of their training, vision for growth, and experience, then those they hire end up lacking these important skills. The other problem with this hasty hiring is that these athletes immediately turn to hiring when something breaks or a need emerges. Some problems should be ignored in the early stages.

Professional athletes aren't alone in their hiring mistakes. Plenty of businessmen fall into the same traps. Don't assume that just hiring another warm body will instantly resolve your problem(s). You have to know when and how to hire or when to find another solution to your problem. You'll have to study competitors and non-competitors in order to identify the best hiring practices for growth, scale, and organizational development. If you fail to prioritize your hiring plan, you'll either grow stagnant or fail early in the game. Throwing people at a problem is not the best solution. You'll need to put the right people in the right places, have the right staffing structure for scale, and have the right people development strategy.

How many staff members do you need to be successful?

Step Ten:
Assessing Your Finances

Step Ten:
Assessing Your Finances

One of the greatest challenges for many entrepreneurs is having a sound financial plan in place. Lots of people have passion and great ideas but lack the training to align financial goals and projections with those ideas. Poor financial planning can single-handedly destroy your venture before you ever have a chance to establish momentum.

Your financial plan should include your three-year projections for your profit-and-loss statements, cash flow statements, balance sheets, and breakeven analyses. If for no other reason, a sound financial plan provides perspective on your venture's feasibility. When it comes right down to it, you define the success of a business launch by measuring profits left after paying all your operating costs, staff and bills. If you're forming a non-profit organization, you'll define success through target metrics, impact and outcomes. However, you'll still need to operate a healthy financial model if you want to sustain the impact you want to make.

A financial plan also helps you raise capital from investors, partners or funding institutions. You won't raise substantial capital from anyone external to your trusted network without a sound financial plan. Put yourself in the shoes of a potential investor. Would you invest in someone who didn't have a plan to repay you or generate a return on investment for you? If you don't have the skills to develop a financial plan for your business, find someone who does and make them your very best friend for however long it takes you to get a reasonable plan in place.

Sound financial planning gives perspective to your decision-making process and helps you determine what's conducive and possible. Once you've developed a sound financial plan, you can determine what adjustments you need to make to see the success you want.

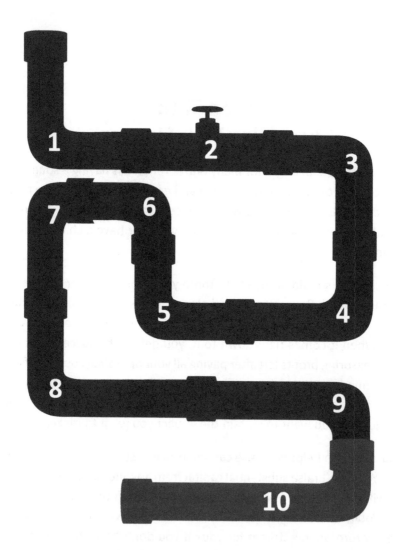

69 | Evaluate Your Pricing Model

As you price your product or service, think about the rule of supply and demand. *Demand* measures the desire of your consumers. The demand determines the *supply* you'll produce. If your product or service has high demand, you'll need to increase your market supply, which allows you to increase your prices.

One of the most fundamental things you can do is look at the world around you. If someone is already selling what you want to offer, benchmark them and take a look at their pricing structure. For example, Gap Inc. has Banana Republic, The Gap and Old Navy. If these brands were gasoline qualities, Banana Republic would be Premium, The Gap would be Plus, and Old Navy would be Regular. You have to determine the "type of gasoline" you're selling. Are you selling ground beef or premium grade steaks? One-ply tissue or two-ply tissue? High quality chicken breast meat or meat made of chicken parts? Once you clarify your target quality, do your research. You cannot study your competitors enough. You'll want to know the ins and outs of their pricing structure. Here is a list to get you started:

- Where do they sell most of their products or services geographically?
- Who carries their products or services?
- Where do the bulk of their customers shop?
- Where do the bulk of their customers live?
- What is the lifestyle of their customers?

Once you know these details, you can determine the best way to price your product for market penetration.

If you want to penetrate a long-existent market, you probably won't win the pricing war immediately, if ever. Your initial goal should be to price your product or service well enough that you can slowly gain market share while increasing brand awareness and credibility. As you increase brand awareness and credibility, you'll increase your distribution options. Better distribution options mean lower distribution costs, allowing you to lower your product prices and still sustain profit margins for growth. Pricing is an art and a science. You have to follow the trends of the market. Otherwise, you'll price yourself right out of business. Many people overprice their products, while others under-price them. You want to find the sweet spot and stay as close to it as you can without growing so counterproductive you implode.

Have you considered your pricing model?

70 | Calculate Your Startup and Maintenance Costs

Make a list of everything you think you'll need to launch your organization or business and count the costs. For example, if your goal is to start a baked goods shop, then you want to calculate every fixed and variable cost you can imagine. Fixed costs can include equipment, machinery, monthly rent/lease, insurance, licenses, permit fees, and other onetime purchases or unchanging expenses throughout your first year(s) of operations. On the other hand, variable costs could include operational undertakings such as technology, research expenses, marketing, advertising, social media, and employee expenses. Other variable costs could include bulk quantities of cookie dough, chocolate chips, eggs, sugar, milk, flour and other ingredients required to run a successful shop. Regardless of the industry, you must consider costs.

Once you've calculated fixed and variable costs, utilize a data analysis tool and spreadsheet application to calculate your expenses for your first year of operations. Ideally, you should do this for the first three years but at least calculate for one year. Inevitably, you'll encounter unexpected expenses. Simply add them to your budget and work on increasing the efficiency of your expense projection and management. In the end, your goal is to get into the 90%-95% range of expected expenses. The closer you get with your projections and ability to execute your plans, the greater your probability of beating the three-year death cycle.

Poor financial management has devastated many great people and great ideas. On the flipside, mediocre ideas have been paired with good financial leadership and outpaced the less-structured great ideas. Work at having an exceptional product offering and flawless fiscal management.

Based on your start-up costs, will you need to get a loan?

71 | Measure Your Willingness to Invest the Necessary Capital

It's one thing to calculate costs, but finding the courage to invest that much requires a different level of discipline. In most cases, developing a concept, starting a non-profit or launching a business requires some upfront investment. Many people start businesses without a surplus of capital, but those people make huge financial sacrifices. I know people who've given up everything. I recently encountered a couple who sold their home, downsized to one vehicle, moved into a friend's garage and took out an $80,000 loan to start a clothing company. Four years later, their business generated more than $10 million in revenue.

Do your research, plan appropriately and do everything you can to generate the necessary capital. Study other models, especially those similar to your venture. Yours will be unique, but you can learn from others who've failed and succeeded before you.

Do you know how much capital you need to start and sustain?

72 | Consider Your Loan Options

If you plan to start a non-profit organization, I encourage you to avoid taking out a loan to launch your venture, unless you have a unique social enterprise that will generate revenues in the early stages. On the other hand, most people take out loans to launch a business venture. If you're like the average person, you don't have access to massive amounts of capital. So receiving a loan might benefit your business launch. There are a few things you'll need to keep in mind, however.

First, your debt-income ratio along with your credit score will influence loan approval, its amount and its interest rate. A credit score of 700+ gives you a shot at the best interest rates. A score of 600+ will likely get you a loan but at a higher interest rate. Finally, if your score is below 600, you might find it difficult, but not impossible, to receive a loan from a traditional lending institution. This is where you might need to consider some alternative options such as investors in your community who have a similar passion and are willing to exchange a financial investment for an equity stake in your venture.

No matter your credit score, you should get to know all your lending options. Traditional options include banks and credit unions. Non-traditional options include funding campaigns, crowd and community campaigns, pitch competitions, and the like.

Look at all your options and find the best match for your venture. Your goal is to get the optimum capital with the lowest interest rate. Keep in mind that the optimum amount might not be the highest amount. You don't want too much capital too swiftly. In a number of cases, businesses that grow too swiftly mismanage and misuse their excess capital, whereas ventures that grow little by little can manage and sustain long-term growth. Don't bite off more than you can chew. Instead of advancing you and your business, this can ultimately devastate you both.

Loans offer a useful and often necessary foothold. Consider your specific venture and decide if a loan would advance the project. If it will, assess your options and prepare your pitch. Before you ask for support from any of these investors, you should know what you need, why you need it and what you plan to do with it. Like any other asset, you want to manage loans with wisdom and preparation.

Are you willing to invest the money needed to start and sustain your idea?

73 | Generate Profit from Your Revenues

Imagine opening a lemonade stand in your community. Let's break down the numbers and determine what it will take for you to generate a profit for each cup you sell. If for each cup of lemonade you pay 10 cents for the cup, 5 cents for ingredients, and 10 cents for miscellaneous and overhead costs, then your breakeven point would be 25 cents per cup. Every penny after that is profit. For a full-blown business, you'd also have to factor in staffing expenses, taxes, equipment costs and other blind expenditures you'll incur along the way. These additional expenses should influence your final price for each cup of lemonade.

So your goal, as an example, might be to determine whether 50 cents per cup or 1 dollar per cup is the optimum retail price. Keep in mind, you're trying to strike a balance between profits generated and market share taken from the competitive lemonade stand down the street. If you price a cup of lemonade too low, you won't generate enough capital to sustain and grow your business. If you price your lemonade too high, your customers will shop with your competitor. Do a market analysis and crunch the numbers so you know exactly what price you can get away with.

The lemonade stand concept simplifies the business, but this example should give you an idea of the process. Take the same steps for your venture. List your expenses per unit, allowing some wiggle room for unexpected costs, and research the prices of your competitors. Then, use this information to optimize your price point.

How much do you need to generate in revenues to make a profit?

74 | Calculate Your Initial Costs

You have to invest everything you can to establish a brand that shows excellence and uniqueness. Don't compromise quality. Until you build brand credibility and customer loyalty, your best chance is to fight to create a WOW experience for every customer.

You have to consider many costs when preparing to move an idea from concept to reality. Some general costs will include an identity package (i.e. logo design, envelopes, letterhead, etc.), a business plan, installation fees, permits, licenses, business insurance, business registration, structural set up (e.g. LLC or Sole Proprietorship), marketing, social media engagement, accounting, package design, packaging, market surveying, rent, and utilities.

Some of these expenses might not apply to you if you have access to *pro bono* support or other resources. No matter your situation, you should identify the expenses that you cannot avoid. These could tie specifically to the type of industry you pursue. For example, if you open a restaurant, you'll have health department regulations and the expenses that come with meeting those regulations. Unavoidable expenses are those that improve quality and presentation.

Enter your venture with the mentality that there will always be more expenses. Overestimate your costs and underestimate your income. This will keep you calibrated and hopefully keep you out of a financially vulnerable position.

What are your initial expenses to get your business off the ground?

75 | Plan Your 3-Year Budget Projections

As you think about developing a budget, think about projecting at least three years out. Three-year projections are important because potential investors and funders want to see that you know what it takes to break the three-year death cycle and build a viable business. If you have experience developing budgets, you're in great shape. If you're like most people and don't have this experience, consider organizing a budget team. This team could include a successful entrepreneur, an accountant, a CEO, a CFO, a bookkeeper or anyone else you know who would be willing to assist you. These people have been trained to do what the average person can't. If you know someone personally, take advantage of the resource. Leverage their expertise. Don't try taking on this budgeting task alone.

You also want to set financial goals. Do a break even, surplus, and deficit analysis so you have perspective in all three categories. Think through your short and long-term goals and make sure your budget projections reflect these. Once you've analyzed these categories, begin developing a budget template. This template should include every line item in your venture, should have a month-by-month breakdown, and should have all your assumptions factored in for all three years. You can use your template for year one to outline years two and three. Then you can add projected expenses and revenues that you don't anticipate for year one.

There are many online templates you can use as benchmarks to develop your own budget outline. You can also refer to books, seminars, CDs, DVDs and other resources. With so many valuable tools, you shouldn't try to budget alone. A great CFO and friend of mine says, "Entrepreneurs should be creative in many areas but accounting is not one of them!" Don't try to be creative in this department. That's how you earn a visit from the IRS. Many businessmen have wrestled with this task before, so learn from them and don't take on an unnecessary challenge. Consult experts who budget for a living and use the available resources.

What are your 3-year budget projections?

76 | Choose Your Insurance

Insurance feels like a waste of financial resources . . . until you need it! Regardless of your feelings, budget for insurance. When launching, you have to determine the amount of risk you're willing to take. This will determine the insurance you need. You have a variety of options, but here are a few of the basics:

- Business Owners Insurance – This policy covers business interruption, property, vehicle, liability and more. You can tailor this type of policy to fit your needs based on the type of business or non-profit structure you choose. In most cases, you'll do better getting bundled coverage instead of having individual coverage for numerous categories. However, do the math and weigh your options.

- General Liability insurance – A general liability policy covers unintended damages if you, your employee(s), your product(s) or services cause damage to a third party.

- Worker's Compensation Insurance – This insurance covers any potential employee who is injured on the job while working for you. Obviously, you won't need this coverage until you have employees on the books. State laws vary, but all states require any organization (even non-profits) with W-2 employees to have workers' compensation insurance. Penalties for non-compliance can be damaging, so you don't want to ignore this law. If you feel you cannot afford this insurance, consider having 1099 (contract) labor on board until you can afford to convert them to W-2 employees. The biggest distinction between these two employee statuses is the way you'll file taxes for the individual and for your business or non-profit organization.

- Directors and Officers Insurance – This insurance protects the directors and officers of your business or non-profit organization against actions that affect the operations and profitability of the enterprise. If a director or officer somehow gets caught up in a legal battle directly related to your venture, this can cover a range of the costs.

- Data Breach – Data breach insurance policies are more important than they once were. This type of policy will protect you against identity frauds by computer hackers.

- Homeowners and/or Renter's Insurance – If you run your venture from your place of residence, you need this policy. This covers both your personal property but also all property related to your venture.

Other types of insurance include automobile, general life, professional liability, and commercial automobile. Research and note the best options to support your launch. Remember to compare companies to find an insurance package that makes the most sense for you. Keep in mind that the insurance agent might look to sell you a cookie-cutter package. Don't allow them to pigeonhole you. If this overwhelms you, use the many resources available to you. Call your insurance agent and get busy deliberating on the best plan for your future.

What type(s) of insurance do you need?

77 | Know Your Tax Obligations

I'm not a CPA or tax collector for the IRS, so I know just enough to be dangerous when it comes to tax obligations for small business and non-profit entrepreneurs. My best advice: Find a competent CPA immediately. You cannot do this soon enough. If you don't think you can afford one, see if you can find one that will do some pro bono work for you and grow with your business. As I warned before, don't be *creative* with accounting. Do everything possible to keep as much capital for you and your venture as possible, but don't cut corners that should not be cut. Exercise integrity and remind yourself you are in it for the long haul. You can get yourself in a lot of trouble if you don't set up an infrastructure that covers you financially.

A few tax implications you want to consider are income, payroll, self-employment and sales taxes. I've spent most of the last decade and a half working with start-up ventures in the non-profit space, so I've dodged the majority of the tax implications facing small businesses and corporations. Now, however, my day is here. With my business partners, we are growing a venture in Southern California. One of our core values is integrity, so we take tax obligations seriously. We refuse to put ourselves in a compromising position that could negatively impact us, our board of directors, clients, customers, and future options for growth and expansion.

Uncle Sam will do everything possible to corner you and get his fair share from you. Limit his share but don't be foolish or unethical. Do your research and sit down with a tax attorney, CPA, or successful entrepreneur.

What taxes will you need to pay for your venture?

Find a **competent** CPA *immediately.* You cannot do this **soon** enough.

Step Eleven:
Constructing an
Implementation Plan

Step Eleven:
Constructing an Implementation Plan

Founders run the risk of coming up with bright ideas but never struggling through the execution. At the risk of redundancy, remember earlier when we discussed the distinction between originators, organizers, and operators? Most people have a little bit of each in them. Others are hard wired in one direction. Know where you are on the spectrum and be honest with yourself so you know exactly how to leverage your first 90 days of implementation. This cannot be stressed enough.

I recommend you begin by outlining your implementation plan. If you're a dominant originator, you're likely thinking, *How boring could that be?* If you plan well and execute that plan, the wins in the end won't be boring. Now is the time to take the thoughts I've shared with you in this book, add it to your other resources, and synthesize your concept according to these principles. Then you can begin building your plan.

This last section will help you with these steps so you can finally charge forward and execute!

78 | Set Your 90-Day Goals

My best advice for your first 90 days is to avoid trying to conquer the entire world. Like a friend once told me, "Don't try to boil the ocean." You can't accomplish all the great tasks you want to accomplish all at once. Small tasks pave the way to the bigger ones. Don't think you can become the biggest, largest, most profitable company in your industry by TOMORROW!

I've seen far too many people start off charging the hill only to discover the climb is far more precipitous than anticipated. If your goal is to launch a hot dog stand, you should begin with basic tasks like identifying a good location. Opening a hot dog stand in the immediate proximity of a 5-star, free-standing steakhouse might not necessarily be a great idea. While this might sound like an unreasonable comparison, people symbolically do this every day when they fail to prioritize properly. For example, other basic priorities for a hot dog stand owner would include securing a name, business license, business cards, and a stand; examining grills; pricing bread, meat, and condiments; and leasing space. As fundamental as these steps sound, not everyone understands they have to address these basics first.

Prior to starting The Gifted Education Foundation, the first priority for me was to spend time with three to five people I trusted to tell me if my idea was realistic. After sharing my vision, I asked them, "Is this a good idea or not?" These people were all high-capacity, executive-level business people who I knew would give me an honest answer. I wouldn't have moved forward without their approval. I was selling to philanthropists and indirect beneficiaries. I didn't have a consumer product or service that I could sell directly to my customer. Because of this special challenge, I needed a body of people to push me in the right direction. Nothing took higher priority because, without that support, I could have wasted a ton of time and energy moving in the wrong direction.

My new project was all about convincing others why they should follow my lead and give students from low-income communities skills for leadership, life, college, and career. I realized others were doing the same work, so I needed to find a way to stand out. I knew the venture would require passion, diligence, persistence and thick skin. I would face a lot of rejection from outsiders, so those on the inside would have to bear that weight with me. I found a crew of thirteen people from all over the country who were willing to sign up for what would certainly be a daunting but worthy task. These individuals became our Board of Trustees and I continue learning hard lessons with them in the trenches with me every day.

Once I secured some strategic partners, I began investigating names for the organization, preparing the website and domain name, and researching how to file necessary paperwork like the articles of incorporation for a non-profit charter and the IRS Form 1023. I had to complete these small tasks first. If I'd started with a logo and brand design, I might have discovered someone else already owned the brand when I went to register. There's a method to the business madness.

These are steps I chose to take in the first 90 days of launching my non-profit organization. Depending on your idea, the people in your circle, your strategy and your steps could look radically different. In fact, in most cases your steps SHOULD look radically different. So don't feel compelled to stick to the script I share here but certainly utilize it as a compass. If you do decide to follow a similar process to mine, you have the benefit of knowing I tried this script and formed a successful non-profit and we are developing a successful business in California.

Take a step back and begin thinking through your first 90 days. Your next step is to write down your goals for those days and begin executing them. If you aren't clear about something, ask somebody. Don't foolishly try to succeed on your own. No need to do that in today's economy when you have access to so many resources.

Once you've written your goals, assign yourself a deadline to complete those tasks. On your list, include both things you would like to do and things you have to do. If you don't include both, you'll tend to do only the things you enjoy. However, you'll likely have a series of undesirable but necessary tasks. Write your goals, create a timeline for completion, and then identify people in your inner circle who will hold you accountable. I recommend you take your list with you everywhere you go and review it frequently so the tasks remain a high priority in your daily responsibilities.

What are your three most critical 90-day accomplishments?

79 | Beat Procrastination in the First 90 Days

Think about the consequences of NOT executing the fundamentals in the first 90 days. I cannot predict all the consequences, but you'll likely face a sense of regret and self-disappointment if you don't deliver on the promises you make yourself. The intensity of that disappointment will vary based on your level of risk tolerance. The risk of stepping out and moving forward with a venture will weigh heavily upon some while the risk of NOT moving forward will weigh heavily upon others. You need to know which of these carry more weight for you and to what extent.

If you decide not to proceed, you should know there is the threat of a dying idea, a potential window of someone else beating you to market with your idea, and the risk that this opportunity might never emerge again. Decide now which will bring you more stress, a failed attempt or a passed opportunity. Millions of people get up each day and kick themselves for letting a great idea pass. I've been in that position and never want to be again, especially when I can prevent such regret.

Work through the due diligence so that whatever decision you make, you can live with the consequences.

How will procrastination impact your success in the first 90 days?

80 | Sacrifice for Success in the First 90 Days

Launching a new venture requires hard work, lifestyle adjustments, and major financial sacrifices. You need to determine what sacrifices you'll make to accomplish the goals you've set.

I'm amazed at the number of people who get up every day and aspire to have the same luxuries that successful entrepreneurs have. They envy their freedom, the cars they drive, the clothes they wear, their homes, their vacations, their social club privileges, and everything else that comes with the territory of being a "wild success." However, many who aspire to have those privileges fail to grasp and mimic the discipline, risks, sacrifices, failures, sleepless nights, and everything else required to achieve what successful people achieve. Like the catchy phrase states, "You see the glory, but you don't know the story."

Don't expect something for nothing. Although you might get lucky breaks, don't build your entire model on them. Don't expect handouts. You have to make more sacrifices and work harder and longer than anyone else around you. While wild things happen occasionally, you shouldn't bet on them. There's no easy way out. There are no shortcuts. When times get hard, take responsibility for the losses. When times are great, give credit away to those who help you construct your venture. You'll battle sleepless nights, stressful life cycles, vicious people, and unexpected events. Still, your dreams are achievable if you set the standards early and prepare to maintain those standards 24 hours a day, 7 days a week. If you don't set the standards in the first 90 days, you'll have a difficult time changing momentum. Begin adjusting now, stick to your guns, and be unapologetic and unwavering in your course. Prepare to sacrifice time, energy, and resources. Then you'll be ready to face Day 91.

What sacrifices will you make in the first 90 days to assure success?

81 | Decide What to Add to Your Life

Many years ago, a buddy of mine decided to launch a hand car wash and mobile detailing business. He hoped to generate additional capital so he could have more income for his family. He worked a typical nine-to-five job Monday through Friday but knew he would have to add some things to his plate in order to see this business take off.

One of the first things he did was add an additional twenty hours each week to his work schedule. He continued his day job, which covered his family's monthly expenses, but added ten hours on Saturdays, six to eight hours on Sundays after church, and some additional hours during the week. He shifted from a forty-hour week to a sixty-hour week. In addition to the added hours, the added work required physical labor in the sun, so he also adjust his eating habits, physical fitness regiment, sleeping patterns, family time, and a number of other things to make room for this new commitment.

The next change he made was to learn about his customers. He knew his target customer had a variety of places to get their vehicles cleaned. So he adjusted his daily activities and spent his time developing and distributing customer surveys, developing market analyses, and executing other steps to acquire customers.

These are just a few examples of lifestyle additions my buddy had to make. You'll also need to add things, ramp up things, and scale things in your life if you want to see success. The way you've been spending your time, talent, and finances in the past will not be the way you spend them in the future. Prepare to add some things to your plate.

What will you need to add to your life and schedule?

82 | Decide What to Subtract from Your Life

Not only will you need to add to your life in order to achieve your goals. You'll also need to subtract some things from your life.

Years ago, the most genuine truth teller I know started a successful landscaping company. Unfortunately, he battled with several addictions that eventually devastated his business. In addition to drugs and alcohol, he was addicted to the approval of others. His business took a series of falls, his family fragmented, and he eventually checked himself into a rehab facility. Despite it all, he did what few others could and re-established his life, relationships, and business. I admire him for his resilience, perseverance, and fortitude to stare death in the face and refuse to let it conquer him. He offers a perfect example of the subtractions one has to make to see success.

You too will likely find some things in your life that could hinder success. Whether your issues are addictions, slothfulness, bad relationships, unwarranted activity, or some other distraction, you have to choose to rid yourself of it. These things don't go away willingly. Bad habits always find a way to rear their heads when you need them the least. Cleaning up the residue of these distractions isn't enough. You have to slice them and dice them until you completely dismantle their power over you.

Whatever your distractions are, call them out, face them, and destroy them now! Don't allow them to continue to reign over your life and prevent you from experiencing the great joy that comes with leading a life-changing venture.

What will you need to take away from your life and schedule?

83 | Decide What to Maintain in Your Life

Your closest family members, friends, and colleagues could probably share a quality about you that no one else matches. What would they share? Maybe you have a gift for relationships that awes people. Maybe you have a natural gift of empathy and matchless listening skills that will make the customer service division of your venture one of the best in the business. Your ability to negotiate with others could be a gift you've possessed since you were a kid hypnotizing your friends into moving at your every beck and call. Now you can transfer this skill to negotiating pricing with manufacturers, distributors, buyers, and other potential clients. If you've always resisted people who don't manage their time well, you'll likely create an efficient work culture your clients will appreciate.

Think about the culture you want to distinguish you from the cultures of other corporate and non-profit environments. Delight in the creation of your culture and lean into it by making your personal strengths and unique gifts a part of that culture. You shouldn't build a culture around your personality alone. However, entrepreneurial leaders have a tendency to infuse a part of themselves into their venture's culture. This is natural and acceptable in the early stages, because if you aren't deliberate in shaping your culture, the culture will shape itself. Culture is happening around you regardless of your attention to it. So you might as well influence it with your strengths.

There's one other pitfall as you begin changing and discarding things in your life. Don't adjust so much that you lose your DNA. Maintain the positive core of who you are, especially when your positive core can add value to the core of your venture. All strengths taken to an extreme can become weaknesses, but don't discard a useful resource. Study yourself, pick the brains of others, and work to keep a healthy calibration of your best qualities. Then you'll remain a beneficial part of your venture's culture.

What will you need to keep in place?

84 | Choose Your Accountability Partner

I mentioned in the introduction that one of the greatest assets I offer is my passion for discipline and execution. Ironically, discipline and execution haven't always been natural for me.

Obstacles, hurdles, inspirations, aspirations and ideas in my life forced me to set certain benchmarks for myself. Ultimately, having my eyes on certain targets inspired me to ramp up my tenacity for discipline and execution. I spent much of my childhood battling to rise above the conditions around me. To do this, I had to fight the temptation to become a *purebred* product of my environment. Even though I'll always carry the fabric of my environment with me, I won't let it blanket me. Pushing against the grain of that world took incredible discipline and fortitude. There were mentors, educators, coaches, and eventual accountability partners in my life that helped move me along my journey. Without them, I could have ended up like many former friends who went to prison, dropped out of school, dealt drugs, and even died.

I was truly blessed to have people who gave me a vision for which I could strive. I wouldn't be where I am today without them. Anyone who believes they're 100% responsible for the success in their life is living in a mythical world. You can attribute every ounce of success you experience to someone else. Whether you were born into a wealthy family, an educated family, or a broken family, others played a part in helping you get where you are today. Whatever you do in life, don't take too much credit for the success. You might entertain a dangerous thought and fool yourself into believing you don't need others to see your visions come true.

Find people who care about your success so much that they're willing to tell you the truth even if it hurts. I've learned so much because I allow people to speak truthfully to me about my strengths and weaknesses. Both are equally important. Without either one, I couldn't make the progress I desire to make on a daily basis.

Include in your 90-day execution plan a goal to identify people you want as your *truth tellers*. You don't know everything about your venture, so you must find people who will support you when you smash into that brick wall you didn't see coming.

You will run into problems. You will need people who are smarter than you to help you solve them. Find accountability partners who will offer you insight as you grow your venture. These people should value who you are now and who you aim to

become. They should have a vested interest in seeing you prosper in every area of your life, not just in the business arena. You'll experience crises that you won't always be able to compartmentalize.

My accountability partners serve on my board of trustees, board of advisors, staff team and in my general friendship circle. I trust each of them to challenge me on business decisions, offer me family advice, or provide me unsolicited feedback in other areas. I realize that if it had been left to my upbringing alone, I wouldn't have had the skills to reach my current position. We need truth tellers not only to survive but, more importantly, to thrive.

Who will be your 90-day accountability partner(s)?

Conclusion

Conclusion

Your success depends on your actions during the first 90 days of your venture. If you don't get the engine cranked and switch the gear out of park, your energy can wane, your commitment can waver and other grandiose ideas can take over. In the end, you'll find yourself right back in the same position you started from prior to reading this book: a place of slow progress to nowhere.

Don't allow the intimidation of moving forward to hinder you, and don't let old excuses hijack your plans once again. Start! Take a step in the right direction, even if it is a small, imperfect step. From there, keep plowing ahead and keep sharpening the ax. Be strategic but start!

Take the time to craft a comprehensive plan of execution that includes 90-day, six-month, one-year, two-year, and three-year goals. As stated earlier in the book, every goal should be categorized within a window of time, speak to a specific category of responsibility, have a very specific point of execution and have a specific date of completion. The following are unique examples of goals that *could* be included in a comprehensive plan of execution:

90 Day Goal:

- <u>Strategic Area of Responsibility</u>: Benchmarking Competitive Businesses

  a. <u>Point of Execution</u>: Develop a White Paper that Describes the Strengths and Weaknesses of my Top Three Competitors

    i. <u>Due Date</u>: On or Before XX-XX-XXXX

Six Month Goal:

- <u>Strategic Area of Responsibility</u>: Branding

  a. <u>Point of Execution</u>: Work with Graphic Designer to Determine Final Choice of Logo

    i. <u>Due Date</u>: On or Before XX-XX-XXXX

One Year Goal:

- Strategic Area of Responsibility: Finances

  a. Point of Execution: Raise $1,000,000 in Start-Up Capital during the First Round of Seed Funding

      i. Due Date: On or Before XX-XX-XXXX

Two Year Goal:

- Strategic Area of Responsibility: Human Capital

  a. Point of Execution: Hire a Minimum of 3 Full-Time, Executive Level Staff

      i. Due Date: On or Before XX-XX-XXXX

Three Year Goal:

- Strategic Area of Responsibility: Funding and Sustainability

  a. Point of Execution: Generate $2.2 Million in Sales with a 20% Profit Margin

      i. Due Date: On or Before XX-XX-XXXX

Aim to have enough goals in place that you develop a plan that positions you to birth, grow and sustain your idea. Yet, don't overwhelm yourself with so many that it becomes counterproductive and you talk yourself out of proceeding. As uncomfortable as this process might feel for you, you must set these plans in the early development stages. Otherwise, you'll be aiming with no targets. You won't achieve anything great by kicking your feet up and waiting for a magical arrangement. You have to get up, get out, and start investing time, talent, and treasures. I leave you with this quote from the ancient Greek philosopher Heraclitus:

> *Out of every one hundred men, ten shouldn't even be there, eighty are just targets, nine are the real fighters, and we are lucky to have them, for they make the battle. Ah, but the one, one is a warrior, and he will bring the others back.*

Now, go. Get to work, WARRIOR!

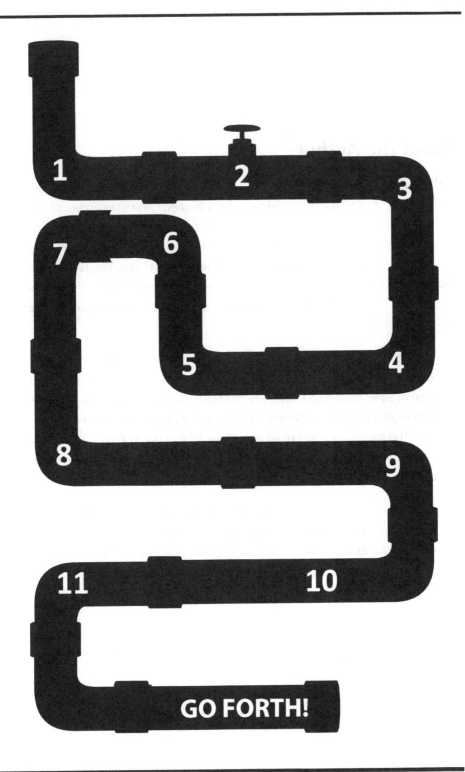

GO FORTH!

About the Author

Anthony Flynn's personal mission is to add value to others through writing, speaking, training and leadership development. As a pioneer and executive in numerous, multi-million dollar non-profit ventures, Anthony has a proven track record of converting ideas and theories to actionable achievements. As founder and CEO of The Execution Pipeline (www.executionpipeline.com) and The Gifted Education Foundation (www.iamgifted.org) along with being a co-founder of Bedrock Creek Consultants (www.bedrockcreek.com), Anthony is actively living out *The Execution Pipeline* model.

Over the last twenty years, he has blazed an unprecedented trail of success in the corporate and non-profit leadership world. He earned a Bachelor of Business Administration in Sales from The University of Memphis and a Master of Arts in Religion from Memphis Theological Seminary. After being heavily recruited or employed by Fortune 100 giants such as Coca-Cola, Philip Morris, Kraft Foods, RJ Reynolds and 3M, he made a courageous decision while still in his mid-20s to devote his career to non-profit and small business development.

Anthony serves on a number of nationally renowned boards and as a consultant to a number of high net-worth individuals, professional athletes, small businesses, non-profit organizations and churches. Anthony loves spending time with his wife, son, and daughter. Additionally, he enjoys reading, physical fitness and mentoring emerging leaders.